Pioneer Missions

Meet the Challenges,
Share the Blessings

Forrest McPhail

Forrest McPhail

1 COR. 9:23

Pioneer Missions: Meet the Challenges, Share the Blessings

By Forrest McPhail

Copyright © 2014 Forrest McPhail

ISBN: 978-1505883183

Scripture quotations are from The Holy Bible, English Standard Version®, copyright © 2001 by Crossway Bibles, a publishing ministry of Good News Publishers. Used by permission. All rights reserved.

Cover design: Michael Carlyle
Interior design and formatting: Adam Wood

Dedicated to my wife, Jennifer, my loving, faithful, gentle, yet strong, companion; my courageous co-laborer throughout this adventure which we call pioneer missions

Contents

First things first.
1) Eliminate Spiritual Component of unexplained or strange "circumstances," Pray & think, Cast out
2) Double Hearty Darkness Hi Ri, MO, 3 km Angkor kingdom
3)

Khmer Romanization

ក	k	ខ	kh	គ	k	ឃ	kh	ង	ng
ច	ch.j	ឆ	chh	ជ	ch	ឈ	chh	ញ	nh,gh
ដ	d	ឋ	th	ឌ	d	ឍ	th	ណ	n
ត	t	ថ	th	ទ	t	ធ	th	ន	n
ប	b	ផ	ph	ព	p	ភ	ph	ម	m
យ	v	រ	r	ល	l	វ	v	ស	s
ហ	h	ឡ	ph,f	អ្	l	អ	a,or,au	អិ	o
អា	a	អិ	e,ek	អី	ey,ei	អឹ	oe	អឺ	eu
អុ	o,ok	អូ	u,uk	អួ	o,ou	អើ	ue,ou	អឿ	uo,our
អោ	aoe	អ្	ur,er,ir	អៀ	oeu	អៀ	ea,ear	អេ	e,ei
អែ	eo,ae	អៃ	air	អៃ	ai	អោ	o,or	អៅ	ao
អុំ	om	អំ	am	អាំ	am	អ្	oam	អះ	ah
អិះ	eah	អេះ	eh	អុះ	oh	អោះ	ah	អោះ	uoh
អុំ	um	អំ	om	អុយ	uy	អួយ	uoy	អ៖	ak
អៅ	av	អៅ	oev	អិប	ub	អុន	un	អ	e
អិះ	ih	អៃ	ei	អាំង	ang	អាំង	aing	អាំង	eang
អាន់	oan	អុ	ua,oa	អាយ	ay	អយ	oi,oy	អ្	I,ik
អ្	y,ee,ie	អុក់	eak	ឥ	e	ឭ	ei,I,e	ឧ	o,u
ឳ	ov	ឫ	roe	ឫ	reu	ឰ	loe	ឭ	leu
ឱ	ae	ឱ	ao						

Foreword

Pioneer ... according to Merriam Webster it is "a person who helps create or develop new ideas, methods, etc. Someone who is one of the first people to move to and live in a new area."

When Jesus Christ spoke the words, "Go into all the world ... and make disciples," He was declaring the launch of a pioneering endeavor! These may very well be the most spoken words in the Church of Jesus Christ, and well they should be since they capture the mission which our Lord left to the Church as He was ascending to glory. Yet there lingers in the heart and soul of every Pastor the questions, "what does that truly mean," and "are we actually doing what He intended for us to do?"

The missionary milieu that we face today has made the possibility of answering these questions with confidence increasingly remote. Even with a passion to see the global dynamic of the Great Commission carried out in tangible ways through the efforts and resources of an individual congregation, yet, still there remain these nagging questions. Too often we look to resolve our doubts by finding answers in the percentage of our overall ministry funds that are directed to "missions," or by the total number of "missionaries" that we support, all the while knowing that neither of these two criterions actually provides a satisfactory answer.

The truth of the matter is that in order for the doubts to be relieved, there must be knowledge that answers questions; truth that clarifies the shadow of doubt. We must both ask and then correctly answer the right questions: What is "missions," and what is it not? Who are "missionaries," and what do they do? What is the "Church," and what is her responsibility? What is the "gospel," and what does the stewardship of it look like? What is a "disciple," and how are they made? What is "patronage," and how can it impair the work of evangelism?

As an experienced Pioneering Missionary in Southeast Asia, Forrest offers us what I believe to be a pioneer work in this field of study. Through the use of clear, practical examples he offers knowledge of the field that we cannot gain from our pulpits and pews. With the light of scriptural truth he chases the shadow of doubt from our practice. Through clear instruction, he offers help for those who would prepare and serve, as well as those who would send and support. I believe that this book offers the Church today a necessary primer for the effective accomplishment of the global dynamic of the Great Commission as we press on to the "end of the earth."

I pray that as you read, your heart will be stirred with missionary zeal. I pray that you will be challenged to apply new commitment to the task of the Great Commission. I pray that you will gain knowledge and embrace truth that will bring new confidence to your practice. I pray that you will be encouraged that Jesus Christ is building His Church and that He is being named in places where He previously was not known. I pray that all of us will be strengthened by the promise that He is with us in the task until He brings us to the end of the age!

Alan Benson

Pastor, Bethel Baptist Church, Schaumburg, IL

April, 2014

Preface

In God's kind providence, my wife and I have lived and served in Buddhist Southeast Asia since 2000. By His grace we have followed the difficult path of many before us, placed ourselves in a position of ignorance and weakness, and have striven to effectively cross cultures in hopes of becoming the best servants of Jesus Christ that we can be.

We have tackled the Khmer language, studied religion foreign to us, and sought to adapt appropriately to Cambodian culture. We have spent many hours pondering the theology of missions and its application. We have put what we've learned to practice in church planting and have observed many other Gospel laborers seeking to work out their individual callings as well.

We have battled physical illness and disease with their accompanying spiritual conflicts. We have suffered defeats, revealing our weaknesses. We have enjoyed flickers of the flame of Gospel power, and we have mourned spiritual darkness. We have had days of great excitement in ministry but have also spent time in the depths of discouragement.

Through all of this, we have often desired a way to communicate what our experiences have taught us to our brothers laboring on fields such as ours, as well as those serving the Lord back home.

During our pre-field and furlough ministries in our native United States, I have come to know many good and faithful pastors who are burdened for foreign missions. These men keep the need to pray, give, and fulfill the Great Commission before their people. Most of these men never have had the opportunity to give serious thought to cross-cultural issues in foreign missions. They were trained to be American pastors, not cross-cultural missionaries. Once these brothers began to be fully engaged in pastoral ministry, they simply no longer had the time to devote much thought to matters other than those issues immediately in front of them.

Missions issues, such as missionary methodology (how missionaries go about their task), are not often explored beyond addressing the need to support the cause with prayer, personnel, and finances. The result for many churches is confusion about what kinds of ministries they should encourage their people to support, and how to prioritize those support commitments. Pastors meet many individuals seeking funding who represent opposite ends of the spectrum in regard to the theology and practice of missions. Funds are limited and pastors do not know which missionaries are best to partner with. Many churches do not have any clear idea about which kinds of missionary activities should take priority in their support commitments. It is for these dear brothers that I write.

Another target audience for this book is the many young men and women (and some older!) who are prayerfully considering taking up the banner of Christ cross-culturally. These brothers and sisters need all the help that they can get in becoming familiar with the issues involved in reaching this world for our Lord. Cross-cultural laborers for Christ face sobering challenges that are often not discussed previous to launching out to do the work. Some of these challenges are unknown to some missionaries until they face them in the very midst of the spiritual battlefield. It is our hope that our perspective will be used of the Lord to help them in their preparation.

Much of this book comes from messages and studies presented in churches during our furloughs and from lectures taught at a Christian university. A number of students and pastor friends have asked me to put those thoughts in print. This is my attempt to meet their request.

To be honest, if I didn't write, I'd burst! While many older and wiser men might be asked to write on these topics, I feel much like Elihu in Job 32 in regard to some topics in this book. Like him, "the spirit within me constrains me .... I must speak, that I may find relief." My heart is simply filled with the need to communicate about some of these matters. They are of great importance to me, because I believe they are important to my God and Savior, Jesus Christ.

I am extremely grateful for my father, Art McPhail, and other godly men of Bethel Baptist Church in Schaumburg, Illinois, that God used to shape my life. I praise the Lord for the gift of a godly and wise father-in-law, Mike Mann, who has pastored faithfully in Sylvania, Georgia, for many years, in spite of much suffering from illness. The Lord used two youth pastors, Mike French and Mike Stalnaker, to keep my feet on right paths and to encourage me in zeal for the Lord. These men, whom the Lord has used to disciple me, are still serving the Lord today and continue to be examples to me of faithfulness to Christ.

I praise God for the excellent Bible college and seminary training that I received at Bob Jones University and Seminary. We have praised God for this many times over during our time on the mission field![1]

We praise the Lord for our mission agency, Gospel Fellowship Association, which provided pre-field counsel, training through their annual missionary retreat, as well as the continually available godly counsel from its leadership who, themselves, are veteran missionaries.[2] Praise the Lord for men like Mark Vowels, Dr. Mark Batory, and the late Dr. John Dreisbach, all serving with GFA at that time, who guided our thoughts and pointed us to good resources as we were preparing for this ministry.

Veteran missionaries J.D. Crowley (currently serving in Cambodia) and Jim Hayes (formerly serving in Thailand) did much to encourage us to dig into the Word of God and think through issues relevant to the pioneer missionary task. Our co-laborer, Chris Seawright (currently serving in Cambodia), did much to encourage my thoughts, convincing me of the need to express them on paper, which ultimately led to the writing of this book. Men like these were used of the Lord to teach me. Some of my missionary friends whom I have met later in ministry have expressed that they did not have this kind of support and encouragement before they left for the field, nor after arriving either. It is for them also that I write.

The content of this book focuses on issues that all missionaries today face to some degree. It addresses some of the privileges, priorities, and problems in connection with pioneer missions through the lens of just one missionary. It is meant to provoke serious thought and study, not provide all of the answers.

In every way that this book accurately reflects the thoughts of God and His Word, may it be a source of strength and grace to His people.

---

1   Bob Jones University, Greenville, SC

2   Gospel Fellowship Association Missions, Greenville, SC

Introduction

Imagine that you are allowed to know one event in your future. In exactly two years, you will be put into a situation where you will have to disable an active, unexploded landmine, one you stumbled upon in one of Southeast Asia's former war zones. You are further told that when this happens, you will have no one to turn to for expertise. You will need the ability to disable that ordnance if you hope to avoid its detonation and your death.

An even greater level of urgency is given to you: not just your life but also the lives of many others will be at stake. This is all the information you are given, and the source is completely reliable. What would you do?

I guarantee that most of us would get acquainted with explosives immediately: what they look like, the various kinds, how they operate, how to disable them, etc. Many of us would start the day we were given this information, zealously learning all that we could. We would read profusely, especially about those kinds of ordnance used in past wars in Southeast Asia. We would want to be ready for the day that we were called upon to disable those explosives, not only for own sake but also for the sake of the lives that will be depending upon us when the event occurs.

I have a confession to make: I know nothing of explosives, though I have seen many indications of landmines in Cambodia and what they can do. My experiential knowledge is limited to Fourth of July fireworks. If I were told of such a future event, I would have some serious work to do! Some reading this might be more acquainted with such things through a line of work or hobbies, but regardless of an existing level of knowledge, all of us would make sure that we were prepared for that unusual event.

There is much more at stake in pioneer missions than lives lost through one major explosion. Our desire to be prepared for this task and to rightly assist its completion should be sobering and fueled by Spirit-driven fervency. However, we must take precaution against haste that is not properly guided by knowledge, for even a passionate zeal for the fulfillment of the Great Commission can become dangerous.[3]

A warning sign in Pailin Province, Cambodia

Former missionary to Cambodia and current Director of World Missions Associates, Jean Johnson, uses landmines to create another analogy. She compares unguided missionary zeal to landmines:

> "When I arrived in Cambodia in July of 1992, there were more landmines in the ground than people on it. Every way I turned, I saw the blatant red signs with a white skull and crossbones warning of danger. The landmines did not discriminate between animal or child, old man or militant. When stepped on, a mine mutilated its victims. Within post-genocide Cambodia, more than forty thousand amputees live without one limb or another, and sometimes without two limbs.

---

3   Prov. 19:2; 21:5

Disfigurement and missing limbs limit a person's mobility. As missionaries, we need to avoid burying missiological[4] landmines. Missiological landmines are ways of perceiving and doing missions that maim the ability of first-generation disciples to multiply disciples among their own people and beyond. It does not matter how many unreached people groups missionaries minister among if they do their task in such a way that those respective people groups do not have the vision and capability to multiply themselves."[5]

In cross-cultural work, and especially in pioneer missions, we must be armed with knowledge before we begin our task lest we become guilty of unintentionally burying "missiological landmines" that hinder our efforts and handicap the national local churches. We must take preparation for our task seriously. Jean Johnson has coined a phrase that encourages us towards that end: "Day 1 affects day 100."[6]

This book is not a how-to manual on pioneer missions. You will not be able to deactivate a live ordnance by its pages, according to our first analogy. It is, however, intended to point out the serious nature of our Great Commission task on pioneer fields, with its accompanying privileges, priorities, and problems.

In accordance with the second analogy, I hope that the truths in these pages will stimulate further discussion and prayerful study so that we might avoid planting "missiological landmines" to the detriment of the national local churches. As many Cambodians know, it is difficult and dangerous to try to raise a crop in a field laden with landmines!

A Few Words about Pioneer Missions

You know you're a pioneer missionary when:

---

4   "Missiology" is the academic term referring to the theology and practice of missions.

5   Johnson, Jean. (2012). *We Are Not the Hero* (Kindle Locations 748–755). Deep River Books. Kindle Edition.

6   Ibid. (Kindle Location 1004).

- Your neighbor thinks that you have magical powers as a holy man
- You suddenly come across a little girl in the countryside and screaming, she runs away from the foreigner
- You apply passages of the Bible referring to food offered to idols to actual food-offered-to-idols scenarios
- Almost every believer you know is a first-generation Christian
- You wonder whether a bag of rice given to someone in compassion might obscure the Gospel
- Many of the new believers confess to having seen demons, even after conversion
- You can quote Genesis 1:1 in a foreign language before you can remember how to quote John 3:16 in English
- When you present the Gospel, you have to address the issue of persecution

While we rejoice in what God is doing in the world as His people strive to fulfill the Great Commission, we must realize that all activities done in the attempt to accomplish this task are not equal. The command to bring Christ to the nations by making disciples requires that we make certain activities a top priority. Pioneer missions is such a top priority. What is a pioneer mission field? In one sense it is true that all of us live on the mission field, for the mission field is indeed the whole world. Some churches even have a slogan above the main church exit that declares, "You are now entering the mission field." This statement is true, of course, but to use the word *pioneer* in conjunction with *mission field* means something more specific. A pioneer mission field is a place where Christ is not named, where Christianity does not have a genuine or felt presence in the society or culture.[7] A pioneer field is one where the Gospel has never significantly penetrated. Many would define an ethnic group as unreached or as a pioneer field if less than two percent of the total population professes evangelical Christianity.[8] In such a place most people have never known a Bible-believing Christian and have no idea who Jesus is or what He has done for them. Dave Doran expresses what must be the Church's passion in regards to pioneer missions:

---

7   Rom. 15:8–24

8   As defined by Joshua Project on their site: *http://joshuaproject.net/joshua-project.php*. In this database, Evangelical Christianity refers to all who profess Christ that do not adhere to Catholicism or a cult. No real standards of faith or practice beyond this are given.

"So, whether the objective is viewed as unreached places or unreached peoples, the burning desire must be to take the gospel to those who have not heard of Christ and among whom there is no viable church planting movement … . We must loudly sound the cry for pioneer missionaries to rise up to the challenge of taking the gospel into unreached frontiers! The territory of the Great Commission is global, and the 'hot spots' of the battle are those places where Christ as not been named."[9]

Some nations that once would have been considered reached with the Gospel have since fallen back into an unreached state because of their culture's later rejection of Christianity. These places are also high priority for missions. They are to be distinguished, however, from a pioneer mission field in that they once were considered evangelized.

Our Perspective

Cambodia is a pioneer mission field. Cambodia's 14.5 million Khmer people and its one million or so ethnic Vietnamese are Folk Buddhists. Upwards of three hundred thousand Cham Muslims form a significant minority as well. Current statistics say that 1.7 percent of Cambodians are professing evangelical Christians.[10] In Pursat province where we last labored, we have estimated that far less than one percent of the four hundred thousand people there are professed believers. The same can be said for our new and current place of ministry, Oddar Meanchey Province, with its 200,000 people.

We have been serving God in Cambodia since 2000, being actively engaged in pioneer evangelism/discipleship, leading to church planting, as our primary activity throughout these years. My experiences include ministry in the capital city of Phnom Penh (metro pop. 2.2 million), the rural provincial capital city of Pursat (pop. 70,000), various villages throughout the

---

9   Doran, Dave. (2002). *For The Sake Of His Name: Challenging a New generation for World Missions*, p. 150. Student Global Impact.

10   This of course represents the widest definition of what it means to be Christian as understood by Cambodian Buddhists. Anyone professing Christianity in any form is included here.

Pursat province, and at the time of this writing, the even more rural Oddar Meanchey province. By God's grace I have become fluent in the Khmer language and understand well the culture in which I labor. My observations about pioneer missions are made through this lens.

God has begun His work in the Cambodian nation. A small number of missionaries labored with difficulty in the early and mid-twentieth century and saw minimal reward for their labor. A work of God began in and near the city of Phnom Penh in the early 1970s as the nation began to fall to the Khmer Rouge, but most of those believers were slain in the ensuing holocaust.[11] Decades of war and great suffering ravaged the people. In the early 1990s the country switched from Communism to "democracy" and capitalism. Along with these changes Cambodia opened up to religious freedom, allowing Christian missions to operate legally and openly.[12]

Many laborers have since responded to the call to preach the Gospel in Cambodia. Most of the local bodies of believers that have arisen are small. Most congregations would feel they were experiencing a great revival if they had even twenty committed teen and adult members. Unfortunately, "rice Christianity"[13] has been promoted by well-meant charity that was used unwisely alongside evangelism and church planting efforts. This has really hurt the foundation of the Gospel that is being laid. Charismatism, as well as the prosperity gospel heresy, has also taken hold among many of these churches. Even still, the word of the Lord has begun to run and be glorified in Cambodia by God's grace.

---

11   A good history of missions work in Cambodia is *Killing Fields, Living Fields* by Don Cormack (Christian Focus Press, 2009 reprint edition).

12   I encourage anyone interested in truly understanding Cambodia, or understanding why this land so desperately needs the Gospel of Jesus Christ, to read Joel Brinkley's *Cambodia's Curse: the Modern History of a Troubled Land* (Public Affairs, 2012).

13   This refers to the practice of obtaining professions to faith in Christ among those receiving physical aid. The result of this practice is that many false professions are made as people seek to secure more material aid by professing Christianity. Those who "convert" under these circumstances are often called "rice Christians." More will be said about this later.

Our Goals in Writing This Book

My goal in writing this book is fivefold:

1. To encourage and strengthen my fellow laborers in the Gospel, particularly those laboring on pioneer mission fields;
2. To give God's people at home a more thorough understanding of what pioneer missions is like on a daily basis so they can better pray and help prepare potential missionaries;
3. To raise awareness among Gospel workers about the necessity of strengthening their understanding in certain areas of theology before they attempt to tackle pioneer missions;
4. To encourage God's people to greater discernment in their support of opportunities to preach the Gospel throughout the world.
5. To encourage God's people to pray specifically for Buddhist Southeast Asia and to send forth more laborers for His work there.

As you read this book you will learn some things about Southeast Asian Folk Buddhist culture, particularly Cambodian, since many of the illustrations will come from our experiences. On the other hand, many missionaries around the world face a situation that is very similar to ours, even though the religious and cultural context might be somewhat different. The same ideas and principles apply in every religious context, whether Muslim, Hindu, Catholic, Buddhist, animist or post-modern. Applications of those principles will vary based on the differences in cultural context, but biblical principles will remain the same in every place.

This book is structured around factors that add to the unique challenges and blessings connected with pioneer missions. There are at least *eight factors* that contribute to the privileges, priorities, and problems faced by pioneer missionaries. We will consider these factors throughout the remainder of the book:

1. Preparatory work is foundational for evangelism.
2. Guarding the Gospel is crucial.
3. Intense discipleship requires dealing with sin.
4. Believers face profound isolation and persecution.

5.   Maintaining New Testament simplicity is crucial for church life.
6.   Misapplications of Bible truth regarding poverty abound.
7.   A consistently spiritual focus of ministry can be difficult to maintain.
8.   Changing times can obscure unchanging needs.

Factor 1:
Preparatory work is foundational for evangelism.

Understand the Farming Analogy in Gospel Ministry

Evangelism on a pioneer mission field *requires* much preparatory work. We can best understand this reality by considering how the Scriptures illustrate the work of the Gospel using farming analogies. It is by no accident that God uses man's experiences in farming to illustrate the ministry of the Gospel, particularly in pioneer missions. Missionaries then must understand and believe the importance of the farming analogy as given to us in the Scriptures.

There are many passages in Scripture that use the farming analogy in reference to the work of the Gospel, and these give us many principles concerning the way Gospel ministry works by God's design. These teach that the work of the Gospel is a process with stages to be worked through before a harvest is gathered. We also realize that pioneer missionaries *introduce* people to God.

The parable of the sower is probably the most well-known of the farming analogy passages. In the parable the Lord compares the various kinds of soils to the different states of the heart among hearers of the Gospel. The sower represents the one proclaiming the message and the seed is the Word of God. The sower is casting the seed widely and generously upon all kinds of soil, hoping for some to take root and produce fruit.

We learn from the parable that people are going to respond to the message being preached in one of the four ways. There will be no harvest without one sowing the seed. The sower himself does not determine the fruitfulness of his sowing, for it is dependent largely upon the type of soil on which the seed falls. Man's responsibility is emphasized here: that of the farmer/believer to cast the seed/the Word of God, and that of the hearer to genuinely receive the message by faith and be fruitful.[14]

In *1 Corinthians 3* the Apostle Paul makes it quite clear that Gospel ministry happens in stages. He emphasizes three: sowing, watering, and harvesting. The seed of the Gospel has already been proclaimed. The seed sown needs to be cared for and encouraged to grow through being watered and

---

"... pioneer missionaries introduce people to God."

---

weeded. Finally a sprout is seen which later results in a fruitful plant. The process takes time, energy, and patience.

Believers in Christ are working together to lead people to God, each sowing and watering as they have opportunity until the harvest of the soul is made when the person repents and follows Christ. Many of us are not desirous of the sowing and watering parts of the process, instead wanting to see the harvest and do the harvesting![15] We must remember also that harvesting does not refer to the production of professions, but to the production of spiritual fruitfulness in individual lives that reflect genuine saving faith.[16]

The account of *the Samaritan woman* and the words of Jesus regarding the people of that district add to our understanding of the Gospel farming analogy. Jesus tells His disciples that the people in that area are like a field that is ready to be harvested. Sowing and watering had already been done in that area and among that people through the prophets and other believers in previous generations. Jesus' disciples did return there later (Acts 8), preached the Gospel of the resurrected Christ, and saw a very fruitful work.[17]

---

14   Matt. 15:1–23; Mk. 4:1–20

15   1 Cor. 3:5–8

16   Acts 26:16–23; 1 Thess. 1:4–10

17   John 4:1–45; Acts 8

Gospel ministry is team ministry. It is God's people working together through time by His grace, faithfully sowing and watering so that some might harvest where others have sown and watered. When we are witnessing, we often do not know where we are in that process.

Mark's Gospel provides us with a humbling illustration regarding Gospel ministry.[18] The Gospel laborer is compared to *a farmer* who does all that he can to prepare for the harvest, only to patiently wait upon God to provide the conditions necessary to secure a good harvest. The farmer does not know how it is that things grow through his labors. He does not cause the seed to grow; he knows only what needs to be done to prepare for a harvest.

So we, too, must do all that we can in this great work and then wait upon our God to work according to His purposes. The key is to do all that we can and *then wait.* Our real helplessness is the emphasis here. We must ultimately trust in God's sovereignty. Yet, if we do not labor, and fall back instead upon the excuse of waiting for God to work, we expose in ourselves a complete misunderstanding of how God has chosen to work.[19]

Like farming, the harvest that is enjoyed will normally be according to the labor expended. Farmers do not have the privilege of harvesting their lands without the hard labor that precedes it. This is the law of the harvest: *we sow, we reap.* This is one of God's unchanging spiritual laws. We must work by faith, realizing that we may or may not be the one to actually see the harvest. Someone else may come behind us and enter into our labors.[20]

A pioneer mission field is like a plot of land that has never been used for farming. The pioneer missionary comes to the untamed land and must get to work so that he can achieve his goal of reaping a harvest. Expecting a bumper crop by means of randomly sowing seed on unprepared soil is beyond reason. Preparatory work, one of the hardest aspects of pioneer mis-

---

18   Mark 4:26–29

19   Someone has explained the thought this way: God has chosen, for reasons not completely known to us, to use three things to bring about all spiritual change: The Word of God, The Spirit of God, and The People of God. God has tied spiritual change to the work of His people.

20   Matt. 9:37–38; Gal. 6:7; Ps. 126:5 (in its secondary application)

sions, is an absolute necessity. The land must be cleared of trees, bushes, and large rocks, and the soil turned up so that the process of sowing, watering, and harvesting can begin.

Human hearts so long hardened by sin and false worship are to be compared to that untamed land the pioneer settler faces when he arrives at his newly acquired property. Unregenerate people on pioneer mission fields require time for their hearts to be prepared to receive the Gospel. Clearing, tilling, fertilizing, sowing, and watering must be done before a harvest can be obtained. This is the work of the Holy Spirit, of course, but He nearly always uses human agency.

One great encouragement to us is that this analogy has limits. Spiritual farmers, laborers in the Gospel, do not share an experience that most farmers face. Occasionally, sometimes all too frequently, a farmer will expend his entire being preparing for a harvest, only to find that the weather works against him and his labor has been in vain. This never happens to workers in God's harvest fields. No word of God returns void. It always accomplishes the purposes for which it was given. The nations will indeed all be represented in that great multitude worshipping the Lamb in Revelations 5. Our labors are never in vain.[21] Praise be to God!

There are complementing truths to consider as well. The apostle Paul expected a harvest through his labors.[22] Some degree of visible fruitfulness was a symbol of the true nature of his calling as an apostle.[23] The gift of the evangelist assumes inherently that God's intention is to use such a one effectively for the Gospel.[24] But it is God alone who can adequately judge the faithfulness of His servants and can measure their true fruitfulness.[25] We must therefore be careful not to judge the servant of another.[26] Every pioneer missionary is responsible to maintain a radical commitment to

---

21   Isa. 55:10–11; Rev. 5:9; 7:9

22   Rom. 1:11–15

23   2 Cor. 3:1–3

24   Eph. 4:11

25   1 Cor. 3–4

26   Rom. 14:4

constant proclamation of God's truth, trusting in God to work according to His will. Our reward from God will be according to our labor[27] and our faithfulness to our calling, not visibly measurable results.[28]

These truths of Scripture must provide the basic framework by which the pioneer missionary operates. If they are not grounded in these truths or if they fail to regularly remind themselves of them, impatience, frustration, inactivity, disappointment, and even despair in their ministry will undoubtedly ensue.

Understand What People Really Believe

Okay, here I am on the field: the pioneer missionary has come to do his duty. I am "super-missionary" with a big SM on my shirt! I have arrived. Now what? Where do I start? What comes first?

The top priority is that I must take very seriously the need to understand what the people believe. I must know what the religion teaches, where that religion differs from biblical Christianity, and what parts of their beliefs already line up with God's truth. How has God already worked in this culture through general revelation? What Gospel truths need to be emphasized the most? How will the people be naturally prejudiced against Gospel truth because of their culture? Where should my starting point be when I talk to people? If I am to seek to build a bridge from their pagan unbelief to an understanding of the Gospel, I must know where to begin. The first question then is, "What do they believe?"

Cambodian Buddhism[29]

The average Cambodian Buddhist's mind has not been confronted with the biblical concepts of one true God, creation, sin as the source of all human

---

27   1 Cor. 3:8–9

28   1 Cor. 4:1–2

29   An excellent and concise explanation of Buddhist religion is *A Christian's Pocket Guide to Buddhism* written by OMF missionary Alex Smith (Christian Focus Publications, 2009). Another is John Davis's *The Path to Enlightenment: Introducing Buddhism* (Hodder

suffering, man's inability to save himself, eternal judgment or reward, etc. For them there is no explanation offered concerning the source of life, the purpose of life, or of any God or ultimate being over the universe.

A Buddhist believes that he must endure nearly endless reincarnations of suffering on the earth until he can achieve nirvana/nothingness/cessation of existence. Buddhism teaches that man can save himself through self-mastery. For a Buddhist, to live is to suffer. Therefore, to cease to live (to end the cycle of endless reincarnation) becomes the very goal of existence, for life itself is the enemy. Through good works delineated by the Buddha one can get closer to the cessation of life. The law of karma teaches that everything that happens to us in life, both good and evil, is directly related to our past deeds. There is no escape from this inflexible law. Buddhism's central tenet is, "You are the only one on whom you can depend."

As believers in Christ, we can readily see major clashes in worldview between the Buddhist beliefs mentioned above and the Gospel. This must inform our starting point for the Gospel. This should also give us a realistic view of our task and how far individuals need to come in their thoughts by God's grace before they can embrace Jesus Christ as God and Savior.

Cambodian Animism[30]

There is a problem with what I communicated to you above. One mistake missionaries often make is that they turn to books written by foreigners in order to learn what the host culture believes, rather than earnestly seeking to understand what the people believe from their own words and practices. Knowing the doctrines of the Buddhist religion is very important as a starting point for understanding what Southeast Asians believe since most do believe in the basic tenants of Buddhism. However, the religion that most Southeast Asians actually adhere to in everyday life is animism and ancestor

---

and Stoughton, 1997). Both of these are written by missionaries to Thailand and focus on Southeast Asian Buddhism.

30   More practical online resources on Southeast Asian Folk Buddhism and Animism can be found at *http://www.cambodianchristianresources.com/missionary-resources/* and OMF missionary to Thailand, Karl Dahlfred's, blog *http://dahlfred.com/en/blogs/gleanings-from-the-field*.

worship. Most books about Buddhism or Southeast Asian Buddhism don't really talk about this, even though it is the real faith of the people.[31]

Animism and ancestor worship are held with stronger faith than Buddhist doctrine for most Southeast Asians. Worship of spirits and demons is found everywhere—spirits of the dead, family spirits, village and provincial spirits, national guardian angels, Hindu gods, spirits of dead national military heroes and kings, malevolent spirits of the fields and forests, etc. Astrology, fortune-telling, and traditional healers are common. It is to these they appeal for the answers to daily life questions, not Buddhism. It does not matter that Buddhism and animism are completely incompatible; logic and reason have nothing to do with the belief system. Often the Buddhist monks double as Buddhist practitioners and healers, even spirit mediums. Superstitious acquisition of tattoos, amulets, and charms are the norm.[32]

Understand How to Present the Gospel in Context

Missionaries must take the time to understand what people *really believe* and then learn how to preach the Gospel to them accordingly. This will usually require the discipline of learning the language of the people you are trying to reach. It should seem obvious to all of us that the most effective ministry is not going to take place through translators. And yet, it seems that fewer and fewer of God's people are willing to devote themselves to a language in order to effectively communicate the Gospel in the heart languages of those on pioneer fields. If the pioneer missionary will take seriously this matter of

---

31   An exception is a small book published by World Vision and edited by Russell Bowers entitled *Folk Buddhism in Southeast Asia* (Training of Timothys, 2003). For a full academic treatment of the subject of folk religion and missions, see *Understanding Folk Religion: A Christian Response to Popular Beliefs and Practices* co-authored by Hiebert, Shaw, and Tienou (Baker Books, 1999).

32   See our concise article on reaching Folk Buddhists in Gospel Fellowship Association Mission's July 2012 newsletter *Sowing and Reaping* entitled "Reaching Buddhists and Agnostics." In it we seek to summarize the points expressed in this book (http://www. gfamissions.org/resources/sowing-and-reaping.html).

understanding the people, it will radically affect the way he/she communicates the Gospel.

Those with this understanding of culture will not use a Gospel presentation formulated in a foreign culture (including popular American Gospel tracts!) and assuming that it is useful where they labor. Why? Because American tracts, for instance, if well-written, address obstacles to faith in Christ expressed in America's own unbelieving culture, a culture which widely differs from that of other peoples like Cambodians. Gospel tracts written for one

---

"Language learning is an absolutely essential discipline required of most who will engage in pioneer missions ..."

---

cultural context also fail to address those questions and potential obstacles to faith that exist in the second culture, making such presentations doubly ineffective on the foreign field.

God has created mankind to require and to depend upon language in order to communicate and understand one another's thoughts. The only way that you can come to really know what another person believes is by speaking their language—really speaking it.[33]

For Gospel laborers, this means that language learning is central for our ability to proclaim Christ to all peoples. As we seek to obey God's command to "be fruitful and multiply" by making disciples among all peoples, we run into this unavoidable obstacle. And yet, this was a part of God's plan from the beginning, and we can take comfort that He will grant us enabling grace to learn languages in order to work out His plan for His glory. What

---

33   At the tower of Babel, God's judgment of confusing the language of mankind forced man to obey God's command to spread throughout the earth (Gen. 11:1–8). This has resulted in the multiplication of languages and cultures, which has proved a curse as well as a blessing to mankind. It is interesting that the Great Commission now compels us to bridge this act of judgment by God's grace in order to unify the nations of the earth in Christ.

a joy it is to meditate on the passages of Scripture which make it plain that Christ's Church will indeed overcome all obstacles by His grace and complete its task![34]

Language learning is an absolutely essential discipline required of most who will engage in pioneer missions, for the curse upon man given at Babel had its intended effect. Genuine discipleship requires heart language-level teaching. Language and culture are inseparable. There are no shortcuts to understanding culture. Anyone who tells you otherwise reveals their lack of a basic understanding of human communication and betrays their lack of experience in cross-cultural discipleship. As Michael Agar explains, "A person is a biographical history wrapped in skin."[35] To get at that biographical history, that culture, we must understand the language that describes and expresses it.

Some might point out that English is an international language, thus making English the best vehicle for fulfilling the Great Commission. I would respond by saying that the vast majority of those who speak English as a second language could not, in my experience, be properly evangelized or discipled through that medium. Most of them do not have the time or opportunity to learn English well enough to be able to communicate with English speakers at a heart level. There may be circumstances when relying on English this way is appropriate; there may be times and places where we spread the Gospel through conversation in English. God will certainly bless His Word, but these opportunities should not be the norm, nor be considered desirable.

One burden that I have had is to encourage Christian young people to aggressively study a foreign language with the hope of being able to use that language later in their service for the Lord. Can you imagine the opportunity for serving God our children would have as they mature, if when they were young they became relatively fluent in Arabic, Spanish, or Chinese? Consider doing a study of a language group on a website like Joshua Proj-

---

34   Acts 1:8; Rev. 5:9

35   Michael Agar. (2002). *Language Shock: Understanding the Culture of Conversation*, p. 238. Perennial.

ect.[36] You will find that people who speak a given language in their home country have moved all over the world. Some of these are from closed countries that have moved to open countries where they could be more easily reached—especially by someone who spoke their first language—and thus understand their culture far better than even the best intentioned others trying to reach them in English.

Just how does a genuine understanding of what people believe on a pioneer mission field impact the laborer's presentation of the Gospel? First and foremost, it brings about an absolute commitment to preparing hearts for the Gospel by laying a foundation about who God is. The best way to do this is to start at the beginning of God's Gospel story, Genesis, especially chapters one through three. Spending much time on creation and the fall of man is the best way to establish an understanding in the mind of the people about who it is that we are speaking of. In these three chapters, many questions are answered that occupy the minds of the Cambodian people.[37] If a person will receive Genesis one to three by faith, they most likely will continue to respond by faith to the rest of the Gospel story. **Genesis 1:1 is *the* foundational truth of the Bible.** Without it, the Gospel has no meaning or value.

Many point out the distinctions between how the apostles preached to the Jews and how they preached to the Gentiles. The key difference was with the starting point. One group was not a pioneer mission field, and the other was. The Jews already believed, or claimed to believe, the entire Old Testament revelation. The main issue for the Jews was whether or not Jesus was the promised Messiah.

Preaching to the pagans was an entirely different matter. Paul's method with those on the pioneer mission field was to emphasize the person of God, beginning with creation. This is clearly seen in Acts 14:15–17, 17:22–32, and Romans 1. Paul and the other apostles knew what every pioneer missionary ought to know today: a person cannot really understand God, sin, who Jesus

---

36   *http://joshuaproject.net/*. This ministry has a lot of useful information for God's people interested in missions. With any source like this, discernment will need to be exercised in its use.

37   As well as all of the other Folk Buddhist peoples of Asia.

is, the cross, eternal life or judgment apart from understanding creation and man's fall. Paul understood, and so must we, that this foundation must be laid if we are to be faithful in Gospel proclamation.

It is no accident that human history from God's perspective (*His story*) begins with creation in Genesis and ends with the new creation in Revelation. The Bible is a story with a beginning and ending, its characters are developed throughout, and conflict is resolved in its pages. Its message is meant

---

"Genesis 1:1 is the foundational truth of the Bible. Without it, the Gospel has no meaning or value."

---

to be understood in sweeping cosmic terms, beginning with creation. In Revelation an angel of God declares the message of the Gospel in such a way that all of the people of the earth hear it in their own language.[38] The passage states the Gospel in cosmic terms as an eternal Gospel, calling upon the nations to fear the Creator God and give Him glory, worshiping Him in repentance. This is the way that the angel addresses the godless pagan nations ruled by the antichrist. He calls upon them to turn in repentance to their Creator and worship Him alone.

Many involved in world missions, and pioneer missions in particular, realize that the best way to communicate the Gospel is to begin at Genesis and build upon that firm foundation. In Cambodia, we have observed that normally there is a significant difference in understanding between those believers who have been taught the Gospel message through something like Creation to Christ and those who have not. In our experience, those who began with creation usually have a better grasp of the Gospel message and of the Christian life in general. This thorough and patently biblical approach to evangelism will naturally and systematically erase the false doctrines of religion and the fears of animism from the hearts of new converts.

---

38   Rev. 14:6–7

Being convinced of this, we must also understand that multiple Bible studies will be required to present the Gospel to people, some taking months or years before they really grasp the Gospel message. **Remember, pioneer missionaries are introducing people to God.**[39] It is true that God is indeed all around them and that they already know some of God's truth through general revelation and the law of God written on their conscience,[40] but they have no knowledge of Him *as He is revealed through Jesus Christ*.[41] The story of Jesus Christ begins with Genesis 1:1.

The great many of the people in the world today are either illiterate or functionally illiterate.[42] Many can read words on a page but have a terrible time with reading comprehension, simply because it was not taught to them. As missionaries have tried to deal with this reality, they came to understand that a storytelling approach was required in presenting the Gospel.

The Bible is one great story of God's relationship with man. Many missionaries have built ways to present Christ that begin in Genesis and use different Bible stories and parables to lead up to the cross. It is absolutely amazing how much theology, how much truth about God, can be taught using just one narrative! This is especially true of Genesis one through three. Other favorite narratives of ours for teaching Cambodians include the parables of the Prodigal Son and the Rich Man and Lazarus.[43]

The unchurched in America are generally not considered a pioneer mission field, but their needs in evangelism are becoming increasingly similar. To be evangelized, they must be told the story of God's salvation from the

---

39   In his book *Building on Firm Foundations: Guidelines for Evangelism and Teaching Believers* (New Tribes Mission, 1987), missionary Trevor McIlwain draws from his experiences as a missionary in the Philippines to show why emphasizing the book of Genesis is so important in missions. We have found that his creation to Christ approach of evangelism, with modifications, to be very effective vehicle for teaching in Cambodia.

40   Rom. 2:14–16

41   Eph. 1:3–14; 3:1–13; Col. 1:15–29

42   Approximately one billion people are illiterate in the world today, not counting all of those that are functionally illiterate, meaning they have very little reading comprehension skill (*http://www-01.sil.org/literacy/LitFacts.htm*)

43   Luke 15–16

beginning, just like those in other countries. There are many now calling on American Christians to realize the need to begin preaching the Gospel by emphasizing the beginning in Genesis.[44] Our Sunday school teachers and other children's workers should have serious convictions about the necessity of laying the foundation of who God is among their students. We must realize the need to speak and teach differently to the illiterate and functionally illiterate. With the ascendance of the digital age, narrative preaching will likely become increasingly important.

Challenges and Blessings to Pioneer Missions

Challenges:

Introducing people to God for the first time and then building upon that foundation will usually require much time and many encounters. Visible fruitfulness may come very slowly, especially in the beginning years of ministry. Pioneer missionaries must be willing to be seed sowers and waterers, even while there is very limited visible fruit. God just doesn't seem to work like the church growth manuals tell us, especially on the pioneer mission field! Missionaries must refuse to water down the message or use marketing to try to create "fruit."

Blessings:

There is great joy found in introducing people to God. This is the greatest privilege that a pioneer missionary has. Watching the illuminating work of the Holy Spirit teach people the Gospel and bring them to repentance and faith in such contexts is a glory to behold. Another blessing is the joy of focusing your thoughts and teaching ministry on the basic truths of the Gospel. In other contexts it is easy to skip past the basic truths and become improperly focused on "the finer things" of theology, thus losing sight of the most important and fundamental truths of our faith.

---

44   *http://creation.com/; http://www.answersingenesis.org/; http://www.icr.org/*

Factor 2:
Guarding the Gospel is crucial.

The Danger of Syncretism

Here is how many Cambodian Folk Buddhists might be tempted to adapt Christianity to their old religion: simply worship Jesus as one of the many beings honored. They could even claim to worship only the God of the Bible, but do so by remaking God into a god like their old gods. They would worship Him only because they understood Him to be more powerful and therefore most able to bring them the wealth and prosperity they desire. They would not worship Him because they knew Him to be the only true God. It would not be because they saw their need to deal with sin and be restored with God through the Savior, Jesus Christ. They might even forsake their other old religion, but their conversion would be false.

Their primary interest in Christianity would be to possess some of God's power over smaller gods, His ability to heal, or His ability to give them material security. Sound familiar? This is similar to Charismatic theology and the prosperity gospel. Syncretism is the reason why Charismatic theology is flourishing around the world today.

We need to make sure that we all understand what is meant by syncretism. Syncretism is the mixing of one faith/belief system with another. It is not the rejecting of one system of faith for another, but the accepting of various parts of both religions and thus creating a new one. Cambodians already do this by mixing Theravada Buddhism, Hinduism, and animism to come up with their current religion, Folk Buddhism. Satan is masterful at encouraging sinful men to pick and choose parts of God's revelation to believe or reject. Truth mixed with error in the name of Christianity is ever the way of the Devil.[45]

---

45   Gen. 3:5; 2 Cor. 10:13–15

Syncretism is a serious danger on pioneer mission fields. We know this because of how both the Old Testament and the New Testament warn God's people over and over again to beware of this sin.

Syncretism in the Old Testament

Israel fell into syncretism at Mt. Sinai even while Moses was receiving the Ten Commandments. They worshiped a golden calf modeled after pagan religion, calling the image "Yahweh/Jehovah."[46] In the law given at Sinai, and in revelation following, God warned the people of Israel repeatedly about this danger before they finally entered into the land of Canaan. The book of Deuteronomy in particular (the second giving of the law), given before

---

"Syncretism is a serious danger on pioneer mission fields."

---

the people of Israel entered into Canaan, is filled with warnings against an apostasy that begins with carelessness regarding God's truth and the acceptance of any form of idolatry.[47]

Rarely was Israel tempted to forsake Jehovah completely, but they frequently tried to serve both Jehovah *and* false gods. The temptation to mix the worship of Jehovah with false gods was far more dangerous than that of outright rejection of Jehovah for another deity. The prophets continually warned of syncretism and cried out against those already guilty of it.[48] One major deterrent to syncretism was simply to remain grounded in the Word of God alone: "Everything that I command you, you shall be careful to do. You shall

---

46   Exo. 32

47   Especially chapters 4–13 and 27–31, which includes much of the book!

48   Warnings against religious infidelity and calling the people of Israel and Judah who have already fallen into syncretism to repentance represents a large portion of the works of the prophets. The sheer volume of God's revelation which is devoted to this issue should cause us to realize the extreme importance of this topic.

not add to it or take from it" (Deut. 12:32). As we read the Old Testament, we see how Israel did not heed these warnings about syncretism. Even its kings mixed the worship of Jehovah with the worship of false gods.[49]

Syncretism in the New Testament

Jesus condemned the Pharisees and Sadducees of syncretism and throughout His earthly ministry warned about those who would alter truth.[50] The apostles made the danger of syncretism one of their primary themes in the Epistles.[51] Guarding the Gospel of Jesus Christ is one of the crucial duties of the church as "the pillar and buttress of truth."[52] Church leaders are called upon to "guard the deposit entrusted" to them[53] and to rebuke those that contradict sound doctrine.[54] This is why loving church discipline must be carried out against those that perpetuate false teaching.[55]

What is interesting about the passages just referenced in the Pastoral Epistles is that they were originally written by the Apostle Paul, pioneer missionary to the Gentiles, to his pioneer missionary co-laborers Timothy and Titus. Pioneer missionaries must guard the Gospel of Jesus Christ that has

---

49   This began with King Solomon, but King Jeroboam became famous as the one king who most encouraged syncretism. The Assyrian colonists of northern Israel did this very openly as well. An account of northern Israel and the Assyrian colonists' syncretism is described in detail in 2 Kings 17.

50   These two religious groups knew much about the OT law and claimed to believe and uphold it. And yet, they neither understood the law of God nor taught it truthfully. They created a false religion built around the Old Testament law.

51   Many passages deal with this, including whole books like Galatians. One primary target of these warnings is the Judaizers who wanted to mix Judaism with New Testament Christianity. Every book of the New Testament deals with the integrity of the Gospel being challenged in some form or another.

52   1 Tim. 3:15

53   1 Tim. 6:20

54   Tit. 1:9

55   As a matter of fact, a church's seriousness concerning church discipline and separation from false teachers reveals its level of commitment to guarding the Gospel. See 1 Cor. 5 and 2 John for examples.

been entrusted to them as they introduce it to new peoples. They must be sure that they preach a sound Gospel message to their hearers on the mission field. They must make sure that those they seek to make followers of Christ really understand God's message! This is why the earlier discussion covered under Factor number 1 was of such foundational importance.

Missionaries can unintentionally encourage syncretism by their impatience.

One particular sin that fosters syncretism is impatience. Missionaries must minister in the fear of God, realizing that they are, above all else, stewards of the mysteries *of God*. As stewards they will be judged for their faithfulness in communicating their Lord's message—or the lack thereof.[56] If we are in a hurry to lead people to a decision for faith in Christ and are willing to pick unripe fruit, syncretism will be one of the by-products. This is one reason why patience is a vital character quality required in preachers of the Gospel.[57]

Sometimes missionaries are tempted to impatience because of personal ambition and the desire to feel and be perceived as successful. At other times it might be the desire to please donors those who have given towards their ministries, many of them sacrificially. Sometimes bad theology drives the impatience, particularly revivalism.[58] If we think our godliness and faithfulness are gauged by *the number of professions* of faith in Christ produced in our ministries, then we are going to be *sorely tempted* to press those who are not yet ready to repent and come to saving faith to make a profession, *inevitably encouraging syncretism.*

---

56   1 Cor. 4:1–2; Jam. 3:1

57   2 Tim. 3:10; 4:2

58   By "revivalism" I refer to that movement which teaches that if we would just be holy and have enough faith, the Church would be in a perpetual state of Pentecostal revival. To those that hold to this teaching, great and visible evangelistic fruitfulness is guaranteed to those believers who will follow the divinely ordained steps of revival. A wonderful book that exposes the origin and dangers of this revivalism teaching is Ian Murray's *Pentecost Today? The Biblical Basis for Understanding Revival* (Banner of Truth Trust, 1998)

Patience and painstaking effort to clarify the Gospel are fundamental Christian character qualities for those seeking to proclaim God's Word faithfully on a pioneer field.

Missionaries can unintentionally encourage syncretism by downplaying the necessity of repentance.

An emphasis on repentance that is Bible-centered is crucial in the protection of the Gospel from dilution and syncretism.[59] Syncretists don't repent. Even if they appear to adhere to the faith externally for a time, they do not turn *to* God *from* sin *to serve* Jesus Christ.[60] Instead, they manipulate truth, adjusting it to their own self-serving purposes.

If we study syncretism as it is described and warned against in both the Old and New Testaments, we should realize quickly that one especially dangerous form of syncretism is a repentance-less revision of true faith in God. In the Old Testament we see that the people of Israel often maintained the sacrifices and rituals but they were still condemned for their lives of sin

---

"Syncretists don't repent."

---

and rebellion against God.[61] In the New Testament we see the Apostles fighting against this false repentance-less Christianity. Some of the clearest examples of this struggle against syncretism are found in 1 and 2 Corinthians, 2 Peter 2, the book of Jude, James 2, and the words of the risen Lord

---

59   Many missionaries have failed to guard against syncretism and some places in the world dubbed "Christian" are filled with syncretistic Christianity, as illustrated in some African nations like Nigeria. American Christianity is also losing ground rapidly to syncretism as God's people fail to stand against false doctrine.

60   1 Thess. 1:8–10

61   The book of Micah describes this false faith well.

Jesus speaking out against it being tolerated in the seven churches of Asia in Revelation 2 and 3.

We have seen numerous professed Christians in Cambodia continue openly in drunkenness, immorality, and even spirit worship. The churches they attend promote this false gospel, which does not include repentance. A pastor in the city where we once lived is well-known for his drunkenness and dirty dealing. Another there is known for extortion and immorality. These and many like them have embraced "Christianity" for purposes other than the Gospel of Jesus Christ, and those other purposes usually have to do with money, prestige, and power.

Wherever the Gospel takes root in the world, Satan's work of sowing syncretism is not far behind. As a result, many professed Christians throughout the world today follow distorted forms of Christianity, mixtures of Christian truth and the philosophies of the world with its sensuality. Every distortion of the Gospel is syncretism, the addition to and subtraction from biblical Christianity. Syncretism selects which points of Christian truth it wants to keep and discards the rest. It is heart-breaking to realize that major religions in the world today have been birthed by syncretism with biblical Christianity, including Mormonism, Jehovah's Witness, Roman Catholicism, and even Islam.[62]

The main idea behind genuine Christian Fundamentalism is to guard the Gospel by resisting and fighting against those attempts by professed Christians to syncretize. Gospel pioneers must be radically committed to preaching and guarding the true Gospel of Jesus Christ. They must work to ensure that their missionary methods do not encourage syncretism or detract from God's message in any way, knowing that they will give an account to God for their stewardship of His Gospel.[63]

---

62   It is no accident that the last revelation of God given to the apostles at the close of the canon of Scripture, Revelation, ends with a strong warning to those who would add or subtract from God's truth (Rev. 22:18–19).

63   1 Cor. 4:1–5

Gospel Tracts

One way to encourage a clear understanding of the Gospel on the mission field is through the use of culturally relevant Gospel tracts. Our missions team here has developed a number of Gospel tracts seeking to approach the Gospel through themes and illustrations appropriate to the culture. These have proven to be helpful, not only in introducing the Gospel to the unbelieving world, but also in clarifying the Gospel to professed Christians.

One of these is the *Ancient Path* tract. This tract seeks to deal with the common Buddhist misconception that Christianity began with the birth of Jesus, thus dating the beginning of the Christian faith to over 500 years *after* Buddha founded his new religion. This tract introduces the biblical truth that Jesus is the Creator God, the eternal God, the God who is over all, who became a man over 2,000 years ago in order to save us from our sins and make us right with Him. Christianity is the continuation of faith in God the Creator that began with creation itself.

Another tract we have produced focuses on the issue of honoring parents. One objection people have regarding Christianity involves the matter of ancestor worship: Christians do not worship dead ancestors. To a Cambodian that means that Christians do not honor their parents. The tract shows how important it is that Christians obey and honoring their parents *while they are still living.* The tract then moves into the Gospel message and the need to honor the God who created our parents.

One Gospel presentation asks, "Why is it that all of the people of the world seek peace and prosperity?" The tract shows where sin and suffering come from and why peace and prosperity elude our grasp. Suffering is a major theme in Buddhist doctrine. Escape of suffering, both temporary and permanent, is the sole motive for Buddhism's creation. It is the universally accepted and spoken motive for all forms of religiosity in Cambodia. Knowing this, we move from this topic to the Gospel. The consequences of sin and the reality of suffering are indeed inescapable in this life. The solution is not to be found in man, but in the Creator God who has provided a way to escape sin and suffering after death: the Savior, Jesus Christ.

Missionaries must zealously look for ways to communicate the Gospel with clarity, looking for themes and illustrations that can appropriately and effectively communicate the Gospel to the people that God has called them to.

One illustration that has proven effective in our ministry has to do with drowning. Pursat City has a river running through it, the Pursat River. The Tonle Sap Lake and the Pursat River supply most of the protein that the people of Pursat consume—fish. Many put food on the table by their own fishing efforts in these bodies of water or other smaller ones. Though many Cambodians fish or use boats, many do not know how to swim. Deaths by drowning are reported often.

In the illustration, we tell of a man riding in a small boat down the Pursat River during the time of the monsoon rains. The water is deep and churning along. Somehow the man's boat capsizes, and he falls into the water. He is alone and does not know how to swim. He flails his arms and legs and is able to stay above water for a little while all the time yelling "Help!" Some people nearby come to the riverside to see what is happening. They see him struggling in the water, and they cry out to him to learn how to swim. They feverishly shout instructions to the man about how to swim, but no one enters the water to help him. This is the way of all of mankind's religions. Religion says, "Save yourself!" The problem is that we cannot swim; we are already drowning and about to die.

Jesus, the Creator God, loves us. We have broken all of His moral laws. We have not sought Him. We have not believed on Him. And yet He came down from heaven to become a man in order to save us from our sins and give us life. Jesus is like a man who enters the water and saves the one drowning. He rescues us from sin and death and gives us life. After saving us, Jesus then goes about teaching us how to live, just like the drowning man was rescued from the water and then needs to learn how to swim. Jesus is the Savior.[64]

---

64   I realize that this illustration has limitations. As someone remarked, "Actually we already have drowned and died. Eph.2:1 A drowning man can save himself by grabbing onto something, or, in desperation, he can make the right movements that enable him stay afloat. But that is not a picture of a sinner who is utterly incapable of doing anything, either to save himself, or assist someone in his salvation … I usually clarify that we are not drowning,

Challenges and Blessings to Pioneer Missions

Challenges:

Missionaries must diligently maintain patience and constantly remind themselves of this danger of syncretism. Learning and addressing the needs and questions of the host culture while remaining faithful to the Gospel can be difficult.[65]

Blessings:

The blessing that this struggle against syncretism affords is simply the joy of seeing God build His church amidst all of the opposition. It is a joy to see new believers, indwelt by the Spirit of God, living out their repentance by applying the Gospel to their lives. When you see His people do this faithfully it is a tremendous testimony to the power of the Gospel.

---

but are like a corpse floating down the river into an abyss of darkness. God takes us and brings us back to life."

65   John Davis, in his book *Poles Apart: Contextualizing the Gospel in Asia* (Theological Book Trust, 1993), provides a good example of an honest attempt to help fellow missionaries to Thailand contextualize the Gospel message. Note: I believe that Davis is extreme in certain parts of the book, but I think that his work is very helpful in making us aware of issues.

Factor 3:
Intense discipleship requires dealing with sin.

First Generation Believers: Lots of Baggage

Have you ever been amazed at all that was going on in the Corinthian church to which Paul wrote? The list of serious issues among them was a mile long. Was this a difficult state of affairs? Of course it was! And Paul treated it as such. However, Corinth was an extremely wicked place. Many were saved from lives degraded by sin. There were some pressing for a syncretized view of Christian living. Welcome to pioneer church planting![66] Many Gospel laborers in pagan pioneer mission fields find themselves being less ready to pass judgment on that fledgling church in Corinth after they have experienced the difficulty of laying the foundation of the Gospel in places just as dark.

Most converts on the pioneer field will be first generation believers. Obviously if a people is unreached or a place is considered a pioneer field, most converts will be the first believers in their entire extended family. Some will be the first Christians in their village or district. They will not have had older Christians to observe in order to discover the Christian pattern of life. They will not have knowledge of many things that are basic to a Christian worldview, knowledge that many in reached places may take for granted. They will most likely have lives that are sin-soaked and scarred. The salvation of some of these will be radical as they have not been converted from within

---

66   This book assumes that readers understand that the goal of biblical discipleship in pioneer missions is the establishment of local bodies of believers who then continue on in the teachings of Christ. As church planting takes place, national leaders must be trained to continue the work. Many in the Church today have strayed far from this simple calling. An excellent work which seeks to call God's people back to a New Testament understanding of the Great Commission is Dave Doran's *For the Sake of His Name* (Student Global Impact, 2002).

Christian homes. The Christian conscience will have to be built from the bottom up.

Lots of Crises

Some areas of Christian growth will take much time to mature in individual lives. One dear woman was saved from a life of drunkenness and superstition. She was also well-known for her foul mouth. When she was converted, her drunkenness and superstition were put off right away, but she found it much harder to do away with angry and harsh speech. This was especially true because her husband stayed a gutter-drunk who later added to her misery by becoming mentally disturbed. The intense pressure every day made it very hard to maintain victory.

A wife came to Christ before her husband. She also came out of drunkenness. She grew rapidly in Christ and voraciously studied God's Word. When her husband came to Jesus about two years later, he was slower to grow and was less studious than his wife. She was very concerned that he was not converted because of it.

Yet, he had fruit of salvation. When she told her husband that she was pregnant, he immediately replied that she should get an abortion because they

---

"The Christian conscience will have to be built from the bottom up."

---

already had enough kids. I remember the day I taught her and other new believers about the sanctity of life. She wept because of the four abortions she had committed before her conversion. Now her newly converted husband demanded that she get another! But when her pastor explained to him that abortion was murder, he readily submitted to the Scriptures. His problem was that his conscience had not yet been informed by the Word of God.

In such situations, discipleship is intense and there are many crises. It will continue to be that way as the foundation of the Gospel is laid. A pioneer missionary has to teach the believers how to follow Christ, and then these in turn must teach one other to do the same in the midst of this mess of sin. It is a battle that no missionary can win in the flesh. Hence the strong appeals to pray for missionaries! We cannot do this. All Gospel work is impossible apart from the grace of Christ, but none more impossible than the laying of the foundation of the Gospel cross-culturally on a pioneer field.

When we started the church in the city of Pursat, most of the new believers struggled with the issue of handling sickness. Physical healing requests dominated prayer meetings. Believers felt that since God was all-powerful and they had endured so much to follow Christ, surely they deserved to be healed from their illnesses. Because of Buddhist thinking, they assumed that every illness was direct chastening from God for sin.

At late 2006, I became very ill from a mosquito-borne illness that left me with a host of symptoms that dominated me for more than a year. My suffering was intense, and the people saw me endure it and continue to minister by God's grace until it took my family off the field temporarily. People kept praying that God would forgive me for whatever sin I was guilty of that caused the illness. As time went on, they began to understand the issues of suffering from a more biblical worldview. The baggage from their Folk Buddhism was slowly being worked away.

Perfectly Equipped

We must carefully apply the Gospel to the culture where we are laboring, keeping the Gospel relevant *without compromise.* We must believe that the Holy Spirit, who indwells the new believers, will help them to apply the Gospel to their own culture.[67] One important aspect of discipleship is helping believers understand God's commands and Bible principles in order to

---

67   Paul was confident that Corinthian believers had all that they needed in Christ to fulfill God's will for them (1 Cor. 1:4–9). He was confident that the believers in Rome could minister to him just as he sought to minister to them (Rom. 1:11–12). He had a high view of God's working in and through the new converts on the pioneer mission field.

make decisions that are pleasing to Him. In this way missionaries work together with God's Spirit to equip the believers to serve God effectively.[68]

In Cambodia, like many other cultures, one of the most important ways by which the Gospel is made both distinct from false religion and also made relevant is during **major life events** such as weddings and funerals. When we had our first wedding ceremony in the church in Pursat, we were most careful—and so were the new believers—to keep the wedding both *Christian* and *Cambodian* without compromise. This took a whole lot of time and thought and hours of conversation. I had to refuse to tell them specifically what to do and kept urging them to be faithful to Bible principles.

When we had our second wedding, even more thought and care was put into the event. Ti, the groom ended up being the primary person to organize the wedding. He sought to retain as many parts of the normal Cambodian wedding that he could while adding Christian symbolism. This was complicated because most things that happen during major life events in Cambodia are laden with Buddhist and animistic ritual or meaning. By God's grace, after many hours of discussion together and Ti working through the issues, he was able to prepare a very Christ-honoring Cambodian wedding ceremony and reception.

One event that Ti introduced at the wedding was a **foot-washing ceremony.** In Cambodia, many perform a ritual for their mothers as they are growing old where the children bathe their mother in a modest fashion, symbolic of their gratitude and respect for their aging mother's many acts of service for them as children. It is a way to show honor. The ritual is not directly Buddhist, so it had potential for being useful to the church.

Ti noticed in John's Gospel that Jesus washed His disciples' feet as an act of humility and love. So the night before the actual wedding ceremony, Ti called all of the family on both sides to come to a special event to show honor to the two widowed mothers. The event provided an opportunity to show public honor for both mothers as well as the opportunity to present the Gospel.

---

68   Eph. 4:11–16

The house that night was filled with people, most of whom were extended family of the bride (Hooie) and were very hostile to her recent conversion. The guests left amazed at how Christians showed honor to their parents, for they saw the believers' sincere desire to love and honor the parents while they are living. This ceremony upheld Gospel truth and was immediately relevant to the context.

Other opportunities for effective witness include funerals, baby dedications, house-warming parties, etc. Christians must have substitutes for these major life event ceremonies, and they must be soundly biblical while also relevant to the culture. This can be quite a challenge, but much less so if the missionaries allow the national believers to exercise their own discernment after having taught them biblical principles. When a foreign missionary tries to plan and direct things that he cannot fully understand himself, confusion, chaos, and embarrassment are unavoidable. When he does so anyway, many mistakes are made and the testimony of the new believers may be damaged.

Loving Church Discipline

We realized early in our first church plant the necessity of beginning immediately to teach God's people about church discipline. When we lay the foundation of the Gospel, those who profess Christ and are added to the church through baptism are expected to live a life that bears fruit in keeping with their professed repentance. This is an essential doctrine for church life. When the apostle Paul was given his command to go to the Gentiles, he saw this as calling people to repentance and expecting those that respond to "perform deeds in keeping with their repentance."[69]

Pioneer churches are not given a pass on this expectation because they are new to Christ; no, they need the teaching even more because of it! Teaching on church discipline is important to basic Christian discipleship because it clarifies what new life in Christ should look like. It clarifies what the Christian life should look like from God's perspective rather than man's. If biblical repentance is taught correctly, church discipline is an important aid in clarifying the Gospel. When Paul gives us lists in his epistles of certain

---

69   Acts 26:16–21

sins that are completely unacceptable for Christians, he makes it clear that continuing in such sin is proof that a person has never come to saving faith to begin with, for these "will not inherit the kingdom of God."[70] Those who choose to continue in such sins reveal that they do not have a spirit of repentance and therefore do not have saving faith. If we truly love God, the Gospel, God's people, and the unregenerate, then we will most certainly actively and lovingly pursue their correction, all the way to the point of church discipline—if need be.

There is only so much we can do in judging the faith of those who profess Christ. God alone sees hearts, yes, but He has given to His church the task of watching over its members to ensure genuine repentance.[71] How does the church do this? When we see our brethren falling into apostasy or some serious and measureable sin, we pursue their restoration and future victory.

> ## "… church discipline is an important aid in clarifying the Gospel."

If those who have fallen make it plain that they are unwilling to return to a spirit of repentance, church discipline is God's dividing of the chaff from the wheat. He chastens His children who need this correction until they return to Him and are restored to the local assembly. Those who do not return reveal they were never His to begin with.[72]

During the first six years of the church in Pursat, we ended up exercising church discipline a number of times: two men for drunkenness; one woman for continuing in Buddhist practices; another woman for evil speaking and gambling; a young man who pursued an immoral relationship and married a Buddhist woman against all family and church counsel; and the Cambodian

---

70   Gal. 5:19–21; 1 Cor. 5:1–13; 6:9–11; Eph. 5:3–8

71   1 Cor. 5:9–13; Gal. 6:1; Heb. 10:23–26; 13:17

72   Heb. 12:3–11; 1 Jn. 3:19

pastor's older brother who would not repent of public cursing, anger and pride which caused great dishonor and shame to the leadership.

One of the men repented and was restored a few years later. The woman who was trying to walk two roads is showing a tender heart towards the Gospel again. The Cambodian pastor and I recently met and spoke about the other man who had fallen to drunkenness and how it was clear that he does not yet understand genuine repentance—and thus neither the Gospel. While we were discussing this man together, the young man mentioned above who married an unbeliever dropped by. The pastor asked if he would consider meeting with him to discuss getting right with the Lord. He has not yet agreed to meet. The older brother of the pastor is in the process of being restored as I write.

Why deal with this? First of all, because God commands us to! Secondly, it has everything to do with laying a solid foundation of the Gospel. Where loving church discipline is not understood and applied, the foundation of the Gospel quickly erodes.

Jonathan Leeman writes:

> "A church disciplines its members for the sake of discipling them. That is, it disciplines them to educate them in the way of Christ's righteousness to help them conform to his image … . An undisciplined church membership is an undiscipled church membership."[73]

We are commissioned by Jesus Christ to make disciples, which results in church planting. If we fail to discipline, we fail to disciple, the result of which is weak, compromised churches doomed to syncretism. Loving church discipline is not optional, especially when laying the foundation of the Gospel on a pioneer mission field!

---

73   Leeman, Jonathan. (2010). *The Church and the Surprising Offense of God's Love: Reintroducing the Doctrines of Church Membership and Discipline*, p. 220. Wheaton, IL: Crossway Books. Leeman's work is a theological defense of the doctrines of church membership and discipline. This book is also very practical. The author shows great awareness of how these issues affect foreign missions as well.

A danger on the mission field is for missionaries to make church discipline a personal matter between the missionary himself and the wayward believer. When this happens, the missionary is the one doing the disciplining, not the church body. In order to avoid this, we have sought ways to deal with these difficult situations in a culturally appropriate way, involving the Cambodian believers at every step. This requires asking them what they think is the culturally appropriate way by which to obey God's Word in these matters.

Much patience, love, and wisdom are needed to work through these situations, and none of us is up to the task apart from a big measure of grace.[74] It is spiritually and emotionally draining, as well as quite inconvenient to deal with sin this way, but it is the only way to guard the Gospel of Jesus Christ in the body of believers. Through this trying process, the love of Christ is made visible. The love of Jesus for His people and also for the yet unrepentant individual is clearly seen. Christian love is also then displayed between the believers in the local assembly.

It is also important to the unbelieving community that they know and understand that we take following Christ seriously. Buddhism in Southeast Asia is mainly cultural tradition for the vast majority of adherents. This was illustrated in a conversation that I had with Pastor Ti in front of two posters which were placed side by side on a wall in a hospital in Surin, Thailand. The poster on the left was full of pictures of various Thai Buddhists performing Buddhist rites and rituals for keeping Thai New Year. Almost every picture included Buddhist monks in their saffron robes. The poster to the right, however, included numerous photos of people partying, drinking, dancing, and being immoral, also in celebration of Thai New Year. In the morning the events of the poster on the left took place, and in the evening the events on the right—and this does not bother most people!

Many Southeast Asian Buddhists assume that conversion to Christianity is merely an exchange of the cultural traditions that one previously adhered to for a new foreign tradition that departs from the ways handed down by

---

74   2 Tim. 2:24–26; 2 Cor. 2:5–11. Notice that in both of these passages Satan is referred to in reference to seeking to obstruct restoration. Through correction we seek to deliver people from Satan. If we fail to forgive those who are ready to be restored we invite Satan's evil influence within our congregation.

one's ancestors. It shocks them to realize that Christians actually discipline members for living in denial of its doctrines! Unfortunately, there are few Christian assemblies in Cambodia today that discipline anyone for anything. In these churches membership has no meaning, and the Gospel has been greatly distorted.

One author comments on the failure of many Baptist churches in America to practice church discipline:

> "One of the most glaring omissions in modern Baptist church life (churches with which I am most familiar) is the regular practice of biblical church discipline. The demise of this practice may well rest in the fact that, by and large, contemporary Baptists have not been taught or do not understand the concept of a New Testament church. The majority of Baptist churches today do not perceive themselves as believers joined together by the bond of the Spirit and associated by covenant in a shared confession of faith in the Lord Jesus Christ and a common fellowship of the Gospel. Contemporary Baptists seem instead to understand themselves as autonomous individuals casually associated together in loose-knit groupings called churches. The concept of a spiritual accountability to God and to one another is lacking or ignored."[75]

Pioneer missionaries coming from cultures that emphasize individualism may have very limited experience and understanding in regard to loving church discipline. One of the purposes of church discipline is to emphasize community, unity, and the family identity of members of the local church. This is something that potential missionaries must think through carefully before heading to the field.

---

75   R. S. Norman. (2005). *The Baptist Way: Distinctives of a Baptist Church*, p. 64. Nashville, TN: Broadman & Holman Publishers.

Challenges and Blessings to Pioneer Missions

Challenges:

Basic discipleship issues require much time and patience. Many serious sin issues need to be overcome, and opportunities for failure are many. Satan is very active in seeking to take down these pioneer churches as is shown so plainly in Acts and the Epistles. Following through and exercising needed church discipline, especially when churches are young and members are few in number, can be a real test of faith. This kind of ministry is both physically and spiritually draining. It is indeed dying daily for the sake of the church.[76]

Faithful and loving discipleship of first generation Christians requires much patience and hope. The missionary must "bear all things, believe all things, hope all things, and endure all things" by the grace of God in order to lead people broken by sin's degradation to healing.[77] We must strive to walk continually in the Spirit's grace while we work through difficult and serious sin issues. We must be especially careful when those sins under question affect us personally, lest we abuse the purpose and exercise of correction within the church.

Blessings:

It is a great privilege to be on the front lines, being used of the Lord to see His work in a place begun. There is great joy in seeing men and women turn away from long-held sin patterns. Seeing the lives and excitement of first generation believers cannot be compared to anything else. When you are placed by the Lord in such circumstances, you experience God's grace in ways you never had opportunity to experience it before. When people

---

76 Much of 2 Corinthians reveals to us the heart of the Apostle Paul who gave his entire being to the ministry of the Gospel. His continual giving of himself was a continual dying to self for the sake of others and for Christ. An important study for any missionary is to trace all of the passages in 1 & 2 Corinthians that refer to Paul's view of himself and his ministry.

77   1 Cor. 13:7

respond to discipline and are restored, the grace of God is magnified to both God's people and those without who are watching.

Factor 4:
Believers face profound isolation and persecution.

Isolation: Religion Integrated into Society

The church of Jesus Christ on a pioneer field is either non-existent or very small. This means that those who come to Christ first in a given area face a very real isolation. This is strongly felt in Muslim and Buddhist cultures where religion is interwoven into every part of life and where religious ceremonies are continual. In Cambodia, every day presents opportunities for ceremonial worship, whether it is the burning of incense to the ancestors or the local spirits, putting food on the altars, giving rice or offerings to the monks, participating in the many religious festivals, or giving offerings to the lay Buddhist elders collecting money for the temple.

New believers feel isolation very keenly if they do not have a local church body with whom to fellowship. Some who have heard the Gospel and have considered believing turn away for fear of this isolation. In general, Asians love large crowds and love feeling like they are one part among many people. Individualism is greatly frowned upon, to a fault, and many Asian proverbs and sayings reflect this. Japan has a proverb: "The nail that sticks up gets hammered down."

Those who come to Christ in this atmosphere need a lot of Christian fellowship, particularly in their newfound faith. This can be hard to accomplish when the believer is the first one in his/her community and when they live far from the other believers.

When it comes time for religious holidays, nearly the entire population takes part. It is indeed religious, but it is also festive, fun, and communal. Religious holidays are indeed integral to culture and community.

This feeling of isolation is never truer for a Cambodian than during Pchum Ben, the Festival of the Dead. Older women busy themselves making special festival foods and enjoying one another's company, the younger ladies and girls helping out. Families go to the temples with offerings for the monks and seek to earn merit on behalf of the dead who may be suffering in hell

---

"... those who come to Christ first in a given area face a very real isolation."

---

or as demons. It is their hope that offerings made will provide relief to the dead who have come up from hell for their annual reprieve. As they offer food to dead ancestors, a feeling of oneness strengthens family ties and relationships. Games, special foods, and exciting events abound, but these are mostly tied to religion or within the walls of the temples. Most people stop working, and many go home to visit their parents. Gambling and drunkenness abound even beyond the already excessive levels of daily tolerance.

The Christian believer, who has recently repented of his sins and idolatry, rightly separates himself from those activities, which are religious. As he or she stands faithfully for the Lord, they find themselves quite alone. The same cycle of feelings and emotions happens at the Chinese New Year and at the Khmer New Year. This feeling of isolation cannot be avoided.

The need for being in good standing with the local church becomes very acute. If a believer continues in sin and is church disciplined, he becomes isolated from other believers and is forced back into the world. Concerning New Testament church discipline, one book notes, "When an individual did not respond to warning(s) or committed a serious offense, it was necessary to effect social isolation."[78]

People who leave the Church hard-hearted find themselves doubly isolated, isolated from the Church and also from the world who mocks them for

---

78   Kurian, G. T. (2001). *Nelson's New Christian Dictionary: The Authoritative Resource on the Christian World.* Nashville, TN: Thomas Nelson Publishers.

their foolishness and indecision. Rather than being welcomed back, they are despised. In Cambodia the world does not readily receive back those who turn to it from Christ. We have seen a number of people who have fallen away and find themselves in a limbo of sorts between two faiths, neither in one or the other. For a person living in a communal society where being alone is one of the worst evils, being outside of both communities is tragic. God's plan for such isolation under church discipline is to drive those who are His people back into the community of faith.[79]

The Call to Discipleship Made Plain

To follow Christ, a decision must be made, a decision that Jesus did not hide from those who would follow Him. His words in Luke 14:25–33 reveal the responsibility of the one who follows Him to make a very serious decision. That decision is to worship Him and place Him above all other people and things in one's life.

When we believe on Christ for salvation, we receive His gift of eternal life, knowing that others may object or even persecute us. We are willing to make family and friends angry, perhaps even losing our relationships with them, so that we might follow Jesus. This means to follow Christ is to choose to love Him more than anyone else.

It also means that we love Him more than anything we possess, for following Him may require that we lose all because of persecution. We may find ourselves alone in the world for our faith. Many have had to make this choice since Jesus uttered these words, and many have faced isolation because they saw the riches of salvation worth it.[80]

In our ministry in one district, we have faced the difficult situation of having three believers in Christ scattered across the large district. Each of them was the first in their entire neighborhood to come to Christ. The pressure on these believers is incredible. We have preached Christ there over the

---

79   1 Cor. 5; 2 Cor. 2:5–11

80   Heb. 11:23–26

course of several years, and no others have yet come to Him. Of these three, one moved to the city of Phnom Penh and faithfully serves Christ there, leaving the nearest other believer more isolated than before. The third, the most isolated, has fallen away, we hope temporarily. Others in that area have expressed a need for conversion but are afraid of the same isolation and so refuse to repent.

One woman in Pursat is the first believer in her whole extended family. She is the oldest sibling in her middle class Chinese-Khmer home. However, she has a slight deformity and has never married. Not only is she despised for her faith in Christ, she is also despised as an unmarried and handicapped woman.

The oldest son in a Chinese home has the burden of upholding the leadership of ancestor worship for the family. If there is no son, the oldest daughter must perform this role. I have had several Chinese-Khmer come close to the point of repentance only to turn away because this burden of leadership in ancestor worship was upon them. They knew for certain that to convert to Christianity would cut them off from their family. The decision is this: isolation from family with salvation through Christ or turn from Christ and escape isolation. Many choose to escape isolation.

Persecution

Persecution is closely related to the last topic of isolation. Persecution, being sinned against and oppressed because of one's faith in Christ, is a real issue in most of the world's remaining pioneer mission fields.

Most places that remain unreached today are Muslim, Hindu, or Buddhist. Many of the Muslim and Hindu peoples are completely intolerant of other religions and are great persecutors of Christians. Some Buddhist peoples are intolerant of other faiths to the point of violent persecution as well, but this is not so much because of religious ideas as it is a fear of political dissidents, foreign influence, or change in culture. In Vietnam, Laos, and Myanmar (Burma) most churches are underground or "walking on egg shells" because the oppression of Christianity is still very real. In Thailand and Cambodia there is religious freedom, and Christians can openly evangelize. This freedom is a relatively new situation for Cambodia, beginning in the early 1990s.

Even with political freedom, persecution of Christians can be intense. Persecution includes isolation, as mentioned above, being cut off from family and friends. At times this is a family decision, not merely because believers cannot participate in religious rituals. Unbelieving families are shamed and publicly humiliated that one of their family members departed from tradition—and thus despise their faith. Some respond by lashing out publicly to try to recover their name. Often the persecution is a reaction to the believer's refusal to be involved in past sins such as drunkenness, gambling, or other vices.[81]

Persecution rarely comes to physical violence in Thailand and Cambodia, but the social shaming can be severe: open ridicule, cursing, demeaning speech, refusal to buy goods from Christians, refusal to attend weddings or funerals of believers, public shaming, being targeted for corruption by the local government, etc. I am unaware of any Cambodian believers in our ministry who have not or do not face continual persecution of this kind. Persecution does tend to lessen over time as people get used to the new faith of their neighbors and see the righteousness that results from it, but it does not cease.

In Cambodia, funerals and weddings are community events. All of the neighbors, much of the community around them, and family and friends from other places converge upon the home where the family is having the wedding or funeral. All are expected to contribute financially to offset the cost of the event. At weddings this is done during the reception. As people leave from the feast they give their wedding gift, which is usually cash. In popular Cambodian culture, the size of the gift is tied to two factors: the social obligation of the attendee to the bride's or groom's family, and how much fun they had, specifically how good the liquor was and how much they drank.

---

81   Peter realized that this would often be the case and told believers not to be surprised (1 Pet.4:1–4).

Grounded Christians in Cambodia, taking their stand on the Scriptures and declaring their faith in Christ, do not put alcohol on the tables.[82] This obedience to the Lord has potentially disastrous ramifications financially. The believing couple's wedding ceremony is already offensive in that it is not according to Folk Buddhist customs. Now the couple withholds from the crowd another opportunity to get smashed—the very reason many go to wedding receptions! How will the Christian's decision affect the wedding gifts? Will the Christian family go into great debt over the wedding because guests feel less obligated to contribute? These are real fears and are a type of financial persecution.

Funerals can also be quite expensive and few Cambodians are ready for such an expense. The community's involvement in helping defray costs is important. When it becomes known that the funeral is a Christian one and not Buddhist, some make excuses not to go and not to give. Others are fearful on religious grounds—the dead are not being honored according to customs, and so there is fear that their spirits will punish the family and anyone participating in the funeral. Some Christian funerals are then lightly attended. Not only is this a financial difficulty, but a source of great shame on the family because it is a clear sign of their rejection by the community.

Persecution is real in much of the world today, going beyond mere words and cursing. This was predicted by our Lord and is a major topic in the New Testament. As the day of Christ's coming draws near, this will intensify.[83] We believers who live in those lands that are yet free politically need to develop a theology of persecution in preparedness for the days to come. So far we have been largely spared, but most of us realize that the situation in our own lands is quickly changing.

---

82 Not only do Cambodian Christians do this for biblical reasons, but another factor is that abstinence from intoxicating beverages is one of the five main Buddhist moral laws. The vast majority of Cambodian Buddhists ignore this moral law and try to make up for it with ceremonies and offerings to the temples. Every Buddhist knows that to drink intoxicating beverages is sin since alcohol affects the mind and causes people to be incapable of maintaining a sober focus on spiritual realities.

83 I encourage you to do a thematic study of persecution and suffering because of the Gospel in the New Testament. Consider tracing these themes in each New Testament book. Such a concentrated study is life-changing. There are far more Scriptures speaking directly about these topics than many believers realize.

Challenges and Blessings to Pioneer Missions

Challenges:

It is very difficult to see many people come to the point of decision only to turn away because of the fear of this isolation. Repentance is costly, especially for the first fruits of the Gospel in a given place. It can be difficult to provide the fellowship necessary to encourage these early believers.

Persecution makes the evangelist face the matter of persecution squarely since everyone knows what to expect if they follow Christ. Once people realize the cost involved, many cease being interested in the Gospel. Many stop listening once the word gets out that the Gospel requires a genuine repentance. The fear of man becomes the greatest single issue hindering people from conversion in many places. Many Cambodians I have witnessed to will confess their desire to study the Scriptures or even to believe, but they are unwilling to face persecution.

It is really hard to watch new converts face persecution. Missionaries can feel helpless because there is not really much they can do to help in a practical way to defray the suffering of their spiritual children. As foreigners, we are not normally subject to the same level of persecution, but pioneer missionaries must be ready and willing to disciple God's people through the many persecution issues they face.

Blessings:

It is a joy to see some who follow Christ and are willing to stand alone, even in cultures where individualism is so frowned upon, because of the prize of salvation. This brings great glory to God. Only God can work in a life to bring them to understand the Gospel and prize salvation this way when the world, the flesh, and the Devil are all weighing in on them in opposition.

Where there is persecution, false professions tend to be much fewer. Having said this, there is unfortunate dynamic in Cambodian missions. In Cambodia there are many false professions, particularly when Christian groups are joining foreign aid to evangelism. Those that profess in this temporary fashion, in order to benefit from foreign aid, usually do not get persecuted like those who profess Jesus Christ in truth. Why? Because these have never repented of their false religion and sin, making their profession to faith inoffensive, except for nationalistic reasons. Also, the Cambodian poor who make such false professions for financial benefit are looked at as merely doing what they can to climb out of poverty. Those who genuinely repent, however, are always persecuted. This reminds us once again of the importance of repentance in our presentation of the Gospel.

Persecution provides for rapid growth in certain areas of the Christian walk. Believers who are actively persecuted value Christian fellowship very highly. The Gospel light shines brightest in times of persecution. The many passages in the New Testament regarding persecution are immediately relevant to the people and reveal the actual blessings of persecution.[84] So many passages of Scripture have a deeper impact upon us when we have experienced real persecution. It causes us to know God's grace in ways otherwise unknown.

---

84   Passages such as Matt. 5:10–12 and 1 Peter are well-used passages in basic discipleship in such situations.

Factor 5:
Maintaining New Testament simplicity is crucial for church life.

Beginning with Acts

We sowed and watered the seed of the Gospel in Pursat province for two and a half years before we saw any harvest. During that time we prayed and planned for the day when God would work. What would we do when those first ones came to Christ? What activities would we encourage or discourage in this new body of believers? What should our role be as foreigners? We were very concerned to keep the ministry of any local churches we started as simple as possible so that the ability of those churches to reproduce themselves would not be hindered. We did not want to create a model of ministry that could not be duplicated by national believers.

Church planting on the pioneer mission field should begin with the book of Acts. When the first converts come to Christ, the missionary needs only to look to the book of Acts and the Epistles for instruction as to how to lead and organize the local church. This is what God intends for us to do, not merely to replicate Christian traditions that were established in other times and cultures. We must keep focused on what the New Testament clearly teaches and exemplifies as we disciple new believers.

Paul, the other apostles, and the apostles' co-laborers give us a paradigm for indigenous church planting. What the NT church exemplified in Acts and the Epistles can be duplicated anywhere in the world, regardless of circumstances. And yet a large portion of what happens in missions today is not remotely similar to the apostolic model—nor is it reproducible by the national believers.

On a pioneer mission field, there are **no traditions yet in place,** whether for good or ill. What the missionary establishes as local church practice becomes the standard through which the new converts understand Christianity and the purpose of the local church. The young church has opportunity to develop Christian traditions that are meaningful to them and appropriate to their own context rather than doing what has always been done elsewhere for reasons that they may not ever understand. The believers on a pioneer

---

> *"What the NT church exemplified in Acts and the Epistles can be duplicated anywhere in the world, regardless of circumstances."*

---

field must be allowed to apply the Gospel to their own context. The missionary must teach God's Word and emphasize its principles, but leave the major task of application primarily to the local believers.

The Four Pillars

We searched the New Testament for Scripture that embodied key activities of the local church, activities that were foundational and essential for local church life and ministry. The Lord led us to Acts 2. Pentecost had come. The Holy Spirit was given to the church. Miracles abounded. Peter and the other disciples preached and prophesied in the power of the Spirit to the many Jews that were there for the feast. Three thousand Jews repented that day, Jews from all over the world. Wow! Every missionary's dream!

The three thousand were baptized, and the church in Jerusalem came into being. Acts 2:42 tells us what the first local New Testament church busied themselves doing. This verse provides for us the four basic elements of local church life. Anything that goes beyond what is entailed in these four activities is secondary in nature.

What are these four pillars? 1) They continued in the apostles' doctrine; 2) They continued in fellowship; 3) They continued in the breaking of bread; 4) They continued in prayer. All four of these are *corporate* activities of the church, what they did *together* in order to worship Jesus Christ.[85] We believe that everything that God expects of His church in corporate worship and service for Him can be put under these four activities. These activities should take preeminence over all else, for as Charles Ryrie stated, "The power of the early church, humanly speaking, was due largely to the facts recorded in Acts 2:42."[86]

We must teach new believers **the Word of God.**[87] Not only do individual believers in the assembly need to keep growing in their own understanding, but they also need to be equipped to lead others to Christ—who then need to be taught.[88] This ministry of the Word of God is primarily done through teaching and preaching, both formal and informal, both in large groups and small groups. Paul testified that this was his primary activity as a pioneer missionary.[89] The other three major activities are vitally connected to this one.

Teaching through singing hymns and spiritual songs is a major avenue for instruction in the Word of God. In passages where God exhorts His people to be filled with the word of Christ, know God's will and be filled with the Spirit—all dependent upon the Word of God—singing is mentioned as a necessary practice in order to accomplish this.[90] Singing is especially effective among the illiterate and functionally illiterate,[91] and is a form of teaching that must be taken seriously. A tremendous amount of truth from God's Word can be easily memorized through the use of hymns and songs.

---

85   John MacArthur refers to these four activities as "the four priorities of the local church" (*Ashamed of the Gospel*, p. 14) and the "four Christian essentials" (*Rediscovering Expository Preaching*, p. 71).

86   C. C. Ryrie. (2010). *Dr. Ryrie's Articles*, p. 19. Bellingham, WA: Logos Bible Software.

87   Acts 2:42 uses "the apostle's doctrine." I am using "the Word of God" for greater clarity as we consider other passages that communicated similar thoughts.

88   2 Tim. 2:2

89   Acts 20:17–38; 5:42; 2 Tim. 1:11

90   Col. 3:16; Eph. 5:15–20

91   Those who are functionally illiterate might be able to actually read words, but they are largely incapable of comprehending what they have read.

We have found especially effective the communication of spiritual truth set to indigenous music styles.[92]

The word **fellowship** does not primarily refer to potluck dinners or shaking hands between stanzas during a worship service, though that is how many in western culture use the word today. The New Testament concept of fellowship has to do with communion and sharing. To fellowship with one another in the local church is to share the same faith and purpose, to have a common bond in Christ. We are to share life with each other as a new family and community and be willing to lovingly sacrifice for one another on both the spiritual and material planes. Fellowship emphasizes being together and strengthening one another. We are to partner together for the cause of Jesus. This is a loving fellowship. It requires time, energy, and material resources. It requires commitment to one another. Pioneer missionaries must strive to help the new believers have this kind of fellowship in ways that are meaningful to their own situation.

God's people must understand the privilege of their new family in Jesus Christ. Fellowship must be known to them as a "bond of common purpose and devotion that binds Christians to one another and to Christ,"[93] a "close association and participation centered around common interests, spending time together, and sharing resources."[94] As Dr. Martyn Lloyd-Jones explains:

"True fellowship is never anything superficial. It is deep. It is vital. It becomes the main thing in life. When people become Christians, they become one. They enter into this community. They are in a

---

92   Every culture has its own music styles, some of which clearly communicate worldliness and sensuality. We must not allow our zeal for being "indigenous" cause us to overlook worldliness and sensuality. Nor must we assume that what constitutes a worldly sound or sensuality in one culture is exactly the same in another. Our desire should be to use local music styles as much as possible, as long as they do not violate these principles of God's Word regarding avoiding worldliness and sensuality.

93   B. Chance. (2003). Fellowship. In *Holman Illustrated Bible Dictionary*. Nashville, TN: Holman Bible Publishers.

94   J. D. Barry, M. R. Grigoni, M. S Heiser, M. Custis, D. Mangum, and M. M. Whitehead. (2012) *Faithlife Study Bible*. Bellingham, WA: Logos Bible Software.

family together. They are united by certain bonds that are indissol-uble."[95]

The breaking of bread is the third key activity of the local church. The ear-ly church often had fellowship meals together, meals called "love feasts."[96] During this breaking of bread in a common meal, God's people shared ev-erything expressing their unity in Christ, regardless of ethnicity or social status. It was to be an expression of love and unity. That is why the Corinthi-ans received such a strong rebuke from the apostle Paul; they were abusing this common meal by encouraging selfishness and inequality.[97]

These common meals/love feasts were followed by worship of the Lord to-gether around His Table. God's people were to publicly declare their faith in Christ and their continued repentance from false religion by taking the Lord's Table together. They no longer drank of the cup of demons, but that of the Lord alone.[98] First Corinthians 8–11 emphasizes to us the impor-tance of the Lord's Table as a *corporate* act of worship. This ordinance must be taken very seriously and not merely tagged onto services as a ritual. Nor must it be relegated in its importance to the individual's edification alone, for this is an important part of *church* life, a part of our *fellowship together.* The pioneer missionary must seek to teach God's people the importance of this ordinance in church life.

Consider how the importance of the Lord's Table is magnified in the midst of suffering and persecution:

> "Look at these simple people meeting together there in the ear-ly church in one another's houses, breaking bread, declaring the Lord's death till He come. Many of them were slaves, very ordinary people having a hard time and being persecuted and maligned, sick in body perhaps, and some sick in mind even. But there they were,

---

95　D. M. Lloyd-Jones. (2000). *Authentic Christianity*, p. 137. Wheaton, IL: Crossway Books.

96　Jude 12

97　1 Cor. 11:17–34

98　1 Cor. 10:20–22

going through this weary, evil world, with the world and the flesh and the devil against them. But they broke the bread, and they remembered not only what Jesus had done but what He was going to do. They lifted up their heads. They said, "We are destined for glory. We are the children of God. We are joint heirs with Christ. We have an 'inheritance incorruptible, and undefiled, and that fadeth not away, reserved in heaven' (1 Pet. 1:4). What does it matter though men kill us, though they revile us, though the whole world be destroyed—we have an inheritance that can never be taken away. It is ours. It will be there until He comes. Then He will take us to be with Himself, and we will spend our eternity with Him in His glorious presence."[99]

The emphasis on **prayer** in Acts 2:42 does not refer to private devotional prayer, but to public prayer, prayer together as a people of God. Corporate prayer, the believers uniting their hearts together in praise, supplication, and intercession before the Lord, is to be a primary activity of the local church. Prayer is not less important than the other three activities mentioned, though it might seem that way by observing church life in many assemblies! It is an integral part of genuine spiritual fellowship. It is also another means by which we minister the Word as we pray according to the Scriptures. The local church simply must know how to pray together, making prayer an essential part of its corporate Christian fellowship. Practical obstacles must not be allowed to excuse its absence.

Corporate prayer must be taken seriously, for "Corporate prayer is the living breath of the church. Through prayer the church resists the assaults of Satan (Matt. 26:41; Eph. 6:13–20), receives the gifts of grace (Acts 4:31), seeks deliverance, healing, and restoration for the saints (Eph. 6:18; James 5:15; 1 John 5:16), supports evangelization (Col. 4:3–4), and hastens the return of the Lord (Rev. 22:20)."[100]

---

99   D. M. Lloyd-Jones. (2000). *Authentic Christianity*, p. 157. Wheaton, IL: Crossway Books, 2000.

100   Kurian, G. T. (2001). In *Nelson's New Christian Dictionary: The Authoritative Resource on the Christian World*. Nashville, TN: Thomas Nelson Publishers.

These four activities are really meant to be interwoven. When we continue in the apostle's doctrine together, whether in preaching/teaching, counseling, conversation or singing, we ought to be actively fellowshipping with one another. The taking of the Lord's Table together revolves around our faith in the finished work of Christ as taught in the Word of God. As we partake together, we fellowship with Christ and with one another. Prayer, too, is fellowship, a uniting of our hearts before God around the truths of His Word in faith. This is corporate worship in its basic and purest form. This is what we must strive to teach the new churches on the pioneer mission field.

A Cambodian House

A traditional Cambodian farmer's home is a small wooden house on stilts. Usually the stilts are made of wood or cement and rebar, with the number of stilts reflecting the size of the house above it. The smallest of this kind of home has four pillars. The roof is usually made of palm leaves or sheets of aluminum. The average sized home is bigger than this and has more than four pillars, usually boasting a large central room with a little bedroom off to the side for Mom and Dad.

What do you think would happen if just one of those four pillars on the smallest kind of home was eaten up by termites and collapsed? What if one of the stilts was knocked loose because of some accident? I have seen houses in the countryside where this has happened. As you can guess, the house begins to sag where the missing pillar was. The house may sag slowly, but eventually the entire house becomes compromised and will come down.

What if two pillars were gone? Or three?

Many churches are really focused on the teaching of the Word of God, but then they fail to encourage a spiritually close fellowship in their assembly. Others take the common meals quite seriously while being almost flippant about the importance of the Lord's Table. Other churches might have a good grasp of the Word and the breaking of bread but then practically despise the necessity of corporate prayer by adding it more as a formality than anything of real importance. It is common for churches to focus on one or more of these central activities of worship and neglect the others.

What we need are healthy Christian churches whose corporate church life is focused on these four priorities. Keep in mind that Luke records for us that the New Testament did these things continually—this was the ongoing lifestyle of the church.

Some might wonder why the Great Commission is not listed as a pillar. I would suggest that the fulfillment of the Great Commission is either inherent in the obedience to the four pillars mentioned above, or the natural outflow from these. A healthy and strong assembly of believers grounded in the four pillars will most certainly live out their faith as witnesses for Christ.

Pioneer missionaries must strive to win people to Christ, organizing them into local bodies of believers that pursue these four core activities together. This is what it means to make disciples. Church planting does not require expensive properties and programs. Local churches do not need all of the

---

"Secondary activities can be distracting, even detracting from the life of a church ... "

---

extra bells and whistles in order to worship together in a way that pleases Christ. Church plants on the pioneer mission field do not need schools, development organizations, or a lot of computer technology. Nor do they need beautiful buildings, musical equipment, or sound systems in order to worship effectively. What they need are these four pillars of local church life. This is the role of the pioneer missionary: to instill these four activities into new bodies of believers and so make of them by God's grace faithful disciples of Christ. All other things are secondary, even if they might be helpful or useful.[101]

---

101 Missionary Melvin Hodges, a missionary of many years in Central America, understood these principles well. His book is full of practical help for how to go about church planting under this simple paradigm: *The Indigenous Church: A Complete Handbook On How to Grow Young Churches* (Gospel Publishing House, first printing 1953).

Secondary activities can be distracting,[102] even detracting from the life of a church for two reasons: 1) They can consume precious time, energy and resources for things that are not eternal; 2) They can give a false sense of accomplishment. Through secondary activities believers can be led to feel that they have really accomplished something of eternal import when those things that are actually of the greatest importance are left undone, such as the difficult and "dirty" work of making disciples.

Adhering to the four pillars makes for a spiritually focused local church life. The flesh does not desire this kind of focus. Even believers will resist such an emphasis at times. Satan will be sure to attack this model. We become sorely tempted to make church life external, program driven, and impersonal.

The simplicity of New Testament church activity needs to be upheld in pioneer missions, not only for spiritual reasons, but also for practical ones. Models of ministry that add to this simple New Testament example require lots of money and expertise, things that most people in this world have little of. Pioneer missionaries must stick to the basics and show the national believers a model of local church ministry that they can easily reproduce in the power of Christ alone.

An exception to this would be ministries that are mainly auxiliary ministries, such as Bible translation efforts and the publication of Gospel and training materials. Such things are immediately relevant to pioneer missions and church planting. People simply must have the Word of God in order to come to Christ and preach His message.

Sometimes there are strategic reasons for having secondary ministries on a pioneer field. Our burden would be to communicate to missionaries that they keep all such ministries separate from the local church ministries that they are planting, especially in less developed places. For example, if teaching English was deemed necessary for establishing a visa or making initial contacts, the missionaries should consider teaching English in a public school,

---

102 By referring to "secondary activities" I am primarily targeting the temptation of churches to fill their church calendar with programs and activities which often distract from what is most important in church life. Busyness and activity, instead of spiritual ministry, can easily become a false gauge of spiritual life in a church.

private home, or another neutral location, and not where the people meet for worship. Why is this? Local church life must revolve around the core spiritual activities and be modeled in a way that is reproducible by national believers. If this simplicity and spiritual focus was maintained, unbelievers would not be led to believe that new Christians have left their former faith to obtain "fringe benefits."

Remember this too—many secondary activities that American churches enjoy are a by-product of a more mature Christianity and greater number of believers. I refer to things like nurseries, age-graded Sunday School classes, facilities for youth events, youth pastors, parsonages, musical instruments, church vehicles, choirs, etc. We missionaries must restrain ourselves from deeming such activities and possessions as foundational in a pioneer setting. The national believers must be allowed to decide for themselves which secondary activities or possessions they would like to add when they perceive the need for them, have the resources to obtain them, and are willing to give.

Whether or not one appreciates the house illustration of the "four pillars" explained above, the fact still remains that the way we do church on the pioneer mission field must be kept simple. Emphasizing this point, J. D. Payne says this:

> "Church planters must seek to understand what is the **irreducible ecclesiological minimum,** or the basic essence of the church, for the church to be a church among any people. It is this irreducible minimum that the church planters must seek to translate to their target group. Anything less than this minimum fails to teach the new believers the doctrine of the church; and anything in addition to this minimum, though not necessarily wrong, possibly hinders the multiplication of indigenous churches."[103]

------

103   Payne, J.D. (2009). *Discovering Church Planting: An Introduction to the Whats, Whys, and Hows of Global Church Planting*, p. 32. Paternoster. This book is an excellent resource for helping missionaries to understand biblical principles of ecclesiology (the doctrine of the church) and how they should impact missionary methodology practically in every cultural context. Payne says, "the most critical issue in church planting today is an ecclesiological issue" (p.40).

Challenges and Blessings to Pioneer Missions

Challenges:

There is a heavy responsibility to establish and encourage local churches that are focused on the essentials. What the missionary does must be reproducible. The missionary must be constantly aware of this need and think through his every ministry decision, considering the implications upon future ministry. If the missionary does not stay centered on the simplicity of the New Testament and imports foreign Christian traditions and secondary activities, he can bring great hindrance to the work he is striving to establish.

It is hard for missionaries sent from well-established institutional churches to go to a pioneer field and keep the work there simple. It is much harder than you might think—which is why so few foreign missionaries really try to do it, even when they know that they should! The pioneer is accountable to God for how he establishes this foundation, because what he does becomes the paradigm. If we would just stick to the Scripture's paradigm, then there would be nothing to fear!

Remember this: the number and quality of secondary activities is not the gauge of success in any ministry. Success is determined by faithful obedience to what we know to be commanded by God and exemplified in the Scriptures, activities like the four pillars.

Blessings:

Starting from scratch and building a church on the foundation of those men and women you or your converts have personally won to Christ is a wonderful experience. Praise the Lord for all who have such an opportunity by the grace of God! Being able to focus on what is really important and redefine local church life based on Scripture alone without wading through Christian tradition is very refreshing and energizing to the missionary's faith.

Factor 6:
Misapplications of Bible truth regarding poverty abound.

Relative poverty and injustice are major concerns on most of today's pioneer mission fields. Many of those yet unreached in this world live in Majority World countries. The less developed a nation is, the more prevalent open corruption, injustice, oppression, and poverty are. Most of the population may live in constant fear of abuse by the rich and powerful. Daily life can be described as barely scraping by to survive.

These fears give the people a fervent desire to climb the social ladder and escape uncertainty and suffering. Many are so tired and worn down physically by illness and the hardships of life that their only thought is survival through the present day. Thinking about deeper things is difficult. Becoming middle class ends up being the ultimate god for many who are relatively poor. Americans or others from more developed nations cannot easily relate to this dynamic.

How is a missionary to operate in a setting of poverty? What is required of a preacher of the Gospel from a wealthy country laboring in a poorer one? Why we do what we do and how we do it is directly related to our theology. If our theology is cloudy or uncertain, then our methodology will be very inconsistent and a constant cause of frustration to us, as well as to the national church.

There are certain theological issues that come to bear on how we as individual believers view our personal responsibility toward the poor, both in our own community as well as around the world. These are topics I've had to wrestle through as I have sought to relate biblically to the economic situation in Cambodia. It is important that all leaders in the ministry of the Gospel tackle these issues thoroughly, or confusion will abound in their ministries. Good Christians will disagree about these things, but we must make decisions. We will look at a few of these.

The Priority of Apostolic Example: How Binding Is It? Does It Matter?

The Apostles, under inspiration, regularly exhorted God's people to be full of good works toward those around them. The Apostles themselves exemplified this by giving of themselves and what they had. For Paul, exemplifying generosity toward those in need was important in proving his sincerity as a preacher of the Gospel.[104] The fact of generosity and hospitality as important qualities for preachers of the Gospel is non-negotiable.[105]

Did the Apostle Paul or any of his co-laborers ever mention that they were anything other than preachers of the Gospel? What do we read about in

---

"If our theology is cloudy or uncertain, then our methodology will be very inconsistent and a constant cause of frustration ..."

---

the narratives regarding the plans and purposes of these men wherever they ministered? The most thorough search through Acts and the Epistles will result in nothing more than an affirmation that their plans and purposes were one: make disciples by going and proclaiming the gospel. Relieving poverty was not their purpose.

Paul knew nothing other than the message of the cross among the people he sought to win.[106] He did help others with his own earnings, so as to be like Christ and to provide an example of what a normal Christian should be like

---

104   Acts 20:34–35; 1 Tim. 3:2–3. As a pioneer missionary it was important to Paul that they not perceive him as greedy or motivated by the love of money. Therefore he chose to refuse any kind of remuneration from new believers or newly planted churches, even though it was within his rights as a preacher of the Gospel (1 Cor. 9; 1 Thess. 2:1–12).

105   1 Tim. 3:2; Tit. 1:8

106   Acts 20:17–35; 1 Cor. 2:1–5; 1 Thess. 2:1–12

in respect to those in need.[107] He gave up his right to receive love offerings from those to whom he labored to keep them from suspecting his motives[108] and to provide an example of a Christian work ethic.[109] But beyond providing an example of Christian giving, nothing is said.

> *"... we must not merely consider what [the apostles] did do, but also what they did not do."*

This is also true for Peter, John, Timothy, Titus, Silas, John Mark, Luke, and all others named in the New Testament as leaders in the fulfilling of the Great Commission. What these men did and what they did not do in the sixty or so years of early church history is vitally important in informing the limits of what we should focus on today. And what the early church exemplified in pioneer missions can be accomplished in the power of God's Spirit anywhere in this world today, regardless of circumstances.

Obviously, the apostles did not believe it was their burden to relieve poverty and solve social ills. Nor do they anywhere communicate that God has given this task to the Church. Missionaries today are not any more responsible to solve societal ills in their fields of labor than the apostles were. Gospel laborers today are called to proclaim the good news of Jesus Christ and be examples of Christianity as individual believers in their community. If a significant believing community rose up in a given place, the culture there would indeed be impacted. Even so, transforming communities is never given as a goal for the Church of Jesus Christ to pursue. Making disciples is our only calling and this must be front and center at all times.[110]

---

107   Acts 20:35

108   1 Cor. 9; Acts 20:17–35; 1 Thess. 2:1–12

109   2 Thess. 3:6–15

110   None of the Great Commission passages communicate anything other than the necessity of making disciples.

When we consider the example of the apostles, we must not merely consider what they *did* do, but also what they *did not* do. Jean Johnson asks us:

> "Why is it that we so rarely talk about what Paul did not do? He did not build church buildings. He did not give out money. He did not start humanitarian projects. Paul did not create institutions and fund ministries to widows, but instructed Christian families and churches to take care of their own widows."[111]

Sok Khim

During dry season we have tried to encourage more aggressive evangelism outside of normal relationship contacts. This has included door-to-door evangelism. The purpose is to distribute tracts, engage the interested, seek opportunities to witness, and find those in whose hearts God is already working.[112]

When we have done this through Inheritance in Christ Church, we go door to door in groups of two or more. For some reason, I was alone on my side of the street when I met Sok Khim. Sok Khim saw me arrive, and she got out of her hammock to receive me. As she approached me from under the shadows of her house, I thought she was an elderly woman. She was not. She was a young woman in her early twenties with three children. She had a huge cancerous tumor that was protruding from her abdomen. Her family, who did not have much money, was leaving her to die. A former prostitute, Sok Khim lived with her parents, and her husband had another wife. When I met her and understood her situation, the Lord made it quite plain to me that we had to do all that we could to try to save this young life.

---

111   Johnson, Jean. (2012, 16 October). *We Are Not the Hero* (Kindle Locations 4800–4802). Deep River Books. Kindle Edition.

112   "Door-to-door" witnessing has been greatly misused in American culture, especially by those who adhere to the theology of Charles Finney. In our ministry in Cambodia, this ministry is not for the purpose of getting professions, but for pursuing opportunities for the Gospel with those with whom we have not yet come to know relationally. Relying on this method as the primary means of evangelism is certainly not wise, but it does allow us one way to obey the command to "go," and some are especially gifted for this approach.

We and our co-laborers pooled our resources, and we had enough between us to take Sok Khim to a hospital in Phnom Penh to have the tumor removed. After the tumor was removed, she began to get better immediately. We hoped that the surgery would leave her cancer free and that she could have more years of life to raise her children, but the cancer returned quickly and there was nothing left to be done. She ended up dying a slow and painful death, but God used us and the people of ICC to be a tremendous blessing to her and her family as we showed the love of Christ. Members of the church began to visit her regularly, bathe her wounds, and show generosity. Her own family and neighbors did none of this for her. Church members sang and prayed with her and encouraged her through the Word of God.

Sok Khim eventually professed Christ and expressed the fruit of repentance clearly. She was baptized in the Pursat River along with other new believers. She died a month later.

The parable of the Good Samaritan in Luke 10:25–37 teaches us that our neighbor is anyone whom we meet in our normal sphere of life, not just our immediate family and friends we would normally care for. Through it Jesus teaches that social class, ethnicity, religion, education, and wealth are not factors in determining who a disciple of Jesus should consider as his/her neighbor. In the parable, the Samaritan showed great generosity toward someone that would normally despise him—a Jew. He did what was within his means as an individual to help the Jew in need, showing genuine love. The actions of the Samaritan show what true righteousness requires of us.

Some well-meaning leaders assume that the application of the parable of the Good Samaritan and the "Great Commandment"[113] to missions is that laborers of the Gospel must make aid and development work an important part of their pioneer missions strategy. Some would even go so far as to say that it was non-negotiable. For these, the simplicity of fulfilling the Great Commission as taught and modeled in the New Testament has been lost. However we apply the Great Commandment, it cannot be allowed to mean that the church needs relief or development organizations in order to fulfill the Great Commission. The apostles and their co-laborers obviously had

---

113   Matt. 22:39

a different paradigm for missions than that promoted in many of the new books on missions today.

I have been asked many times by professing Christians visiting Cambodia what it is that we are doing here. I answer by saying, "We preach the Gospel of Jesus Christ, seek to plant churches, and train national pastors in the Word of God."

My reply often causes them to look confused or even skeptical. Why do so many of God's people react this way? Many Christians have been taught to equate foreign missions with social action and economic development. They assume my answer will be along these lines. Some have even been visibly angered by my simple and biblical response!

Those of us actively engaging in missions simply must face the question squarely and thoroughly—how much liberty do we really have in departing from New Testament example? Our view of inspiration and the integrity of the Scriptures should also help us in forming our conclusions.

Kingdom Confusion: What Is the Gospel of the Kingdom?

Confusion reigns in the Church as to the meaning of the kingdom of God and how it relates to believers today. Do Christians bring in God's kingdom through its impact on society? Is the kingdom of God as promised to Israel in the Old Testament being fulfilled today through the Church? Are the kingdom promises in the Old Testament to Israel being partially fulfilled in the Church ("already-not-yet"), or are those prophecies entirely or primarily still future? How we answer this question regarding the kingdom of God will determine how we view the role of the Church in the world today. Our answer will also inform how we define the fulfillment of the Great Commission. This doctrinal issue is immediately relevant to the topic of missions.

Confusion about the kingdom of God has created a real dilemma in modern missions. Some ideas concerning the kingdom and what it means for the Church today have turned many Christians away from its primary task of proclamation. Many are taught that the Church is called by God to transform society and reclaim the world for the kingdom of God. They believe that the Church of Christ is given a twin calling by God, one which is socio-political/material, and the other spiritual. In their minds, these two are inseparable for kingdom work.

Clearly many today have lost the concept of what it means to labor for the Gospel as the New Testament plainly portrays. The primary need in pioneer missions is for men and women who are separated unto the Gospel to proclaim Christ.[114] Precious few of those designated as Gospel laborers are really devoted to proclamation and disciple-making, because the task of the Church of Christ has now been defined as encompassing so much more on an institutional level.

There are places and times for compassion ministry. There are indeed opportunities for God's people who are not preachers to get involved in cross-cultural ministry (more of this will be discussed below). There may be times when preachers of the Gospel use some form of compassion ministry during their missionary service while they also proclaim Christ and make disciples.[115] The Great Commission, however, is about making disciples through proclamation and teaching. This is the only part of the work that is commanded and exemplified in the missionary work of the apostles. Can I go as far as to say that development specialists are not even on the radar of New Testament priorities concerning the Great Commission?

Is it true that Jesus Christ is "bringing in a kingdom of righteousness, justice, and peace"[116] in part through the charitable contributions and social action of Christians? Is it true that if Christians do not mobilize for institutionalized poverty alleviation that they fail to have a "Christ-centered, fully

---

114   A very profitable study is to trace all of the words used in the NT to describe the ministry and activity of the apostles and their co-laborers. It does not take long to realize that proclamation was central to their life and ministry.

115   For example, church planting medical missionaries who use their medical skills to obtain access into otherwise restricted access nations.

116   Corbett, Steve and Fickert, Brian. (2009). *When Helping Hurts: How to Alleviate Poverty Without Hurting the Poor ... And Yourself,* p. 42. Chicago, IL: Moody Press.

orbed perspective of the kingdom"?[117] If we focus our missions efforts on saving souls instead of poverty alleviation, are we "lacking an appreciation of the comprehensive implications of the kingdom of God"?[118] When the lost world sees the church, are they supposed to see Jesus whose "kingdom is bringing healing for every speck of the universe"[119] by seeing how churches aggressively seek to relieve poverty throughout the world?[120] This view of the church and missions is mainstream today. Is it right? Is it biblically sound?

I believe that those whose view of the kingdom encompasses the Church as an institution solving social ills and striving to change pagan cultures must fall back upon the old covenant, appeal to the theocracy of Old Testament Israel, or use prophecies concerning Israel's future and the Millennium and apply them to today's Church. Only by using replacement theology can God's people appeal to such arguments.[121]

We see that the differences between Covenant and Dispensational theology come to bear on this. One's view of the distinction between Israel and the Church, the future of Israel, and a literal reign of Christ on earth in the Millennium affects their view of the institutional Church's role in society during this current age of grace. Therefore these theological views also speak directly to the issue of missionary methodology. I am moderately Dispensational in my views and this understanding informs my conclusions throughout

---

117   Ibid., p.45.

118   Ibid., p.47.

119   Ibid., p.41.

120   In this paragraph I have stated strong disagreement with the theology presented in When Helping Hurts. My disagreement does not erase my appreciation for their honest attempt to teach God's people better ways to help the poor by avoiding paternalism. In trying to do this, however, the authors provide me with another illustration of how utterly complex it is to achieve the ends that they have in view. The Great Commission is not meant by our Lord to be this complicated.

121   Those who embrace replacement theology hold the view that the Church has effectively replaced Israel as God's covenant people. Therefore, anything that was promised to Israel is now promised only to the Church. Therefore, when trying to define the role of the Church in the world, adherents turn to the Old Testament prophets. Another term used to describe this view is "supercessionism."

this book.[122] I raise this issue here because I think that many who see a clear distinction between Israel and the Church, and who believe in Christ's future literal Millennial reign, do not really understand how those promoting replacement theology have influenced their view of missions.

Our views about eschatology have (or should have) direct impact on our philosophy of missions: Jesse Johnson explains:

> "But I am not convinced that this is really a debate about the nature of mercy ministry or even what exactly is entailed by generous justice. The main theological principle involved is eschatology, and particularly the nature of the kingdom. That is why I actually am not bothered when an amillennialist or postmillennialist argues that the church has a mandate to reform the culture and to combat poverty, because their reasoning usually leads to that conclusion. It is when the premillenialist thinks that way that I see the theological disconnect."[123]

This is not to say that all non-Dispensationalists fall into the thinking that mercy ministry is integral to the fulfillment of the Great Commission. As Jesse Johnson again observes:

> "For those who see the kingdom as entirely future, kingdom work is made up solely of the verbal proclamation of the gospel. This view of kingdom work is not unique to dispensationalists, but is shared by amillenialists who see mercy ministry as an individual mandate (such as Horton), and also those who are skeptical about the church's attempts to right social wrongs in the culture."[124]

---

122   Michael Vlach also has some well-written and concise material showing the important distinctions between Dispensationalism and Covenant Theology (Replacement Theology), both in print and on his blog: *Dispensationalism: Essential Beliefs and Common Myths* (Theological Studies Press, 2008), *Has the Church Replaced Israel?* (B & H Academic, 2010), and his blog at *http://www.mikevlach.com.*

123   Jesse Johnson on the blog *Cripplegate http://thecripplegate.com/,* "Mercy Ministry is Not Kingdom Work" (Sept. 27, 2011).

124   Jesse Johnson on the blog *Cripplegate http://thecripplegate.com/,* "Mercy Ministry is Not Kingdom Work" (Sept. 27, 2011).

Many churches have a mission program that is quite inconsistent with its theology and teaching, and yet this inconsistency goes largely unnoticed. We missionaries cannot help but notice this inconsistency when traveling to churches back home. At times we share conferences with missionaries who communicate almost the exact opposite message about missions ministry than we ourselves express.

Often churches have bulletin boards dedicated to encouraging prayer for the various mission works that are supported by the church. Sometimes we see on these bulletin boards that one local church supports various missionaries and organizations representing very conflicting views of the task. Believers in those churches are being presented with greatly different ideas concerning the Great Commission, the role of missionaries, the identity of

---

"We need to know where to draw the lines in our methodology based upon our theology."

---

missionaries, and what their role as a local church is in this world. Does this tension go unnoticed because the churches think that the Bible gives no direction for them in regards to the accomplishment of the Great Commission? Do their leaders place the fulfillment of the Great Commission in the "anything goes" category?

It seems that few pastors give careful thought to the ramifications of their theology on missions involvement and practice. There are certain views of the kingdom of God that naturally lead to a social work paradigm of ministry, and there are others that keep the Church from that path. If we are going to take the Great Commission seriously, and especially if we are going to be among those that "go" to the nations, we simply must have our theological grid clearly in place and understand its application to missionary practice before we get started in the work. We need to know where to draw the lines in our methodology based upon our theology. If we fail to do this, we enter upon the most sobering of all tasks without map or compass.

Rolland McCune states it plainly:

"There is quite obviously a definite correlation between one's eschatological scheme and any present social engagement in the name of Christ and His church."[125]

I agree.

It is my hope that some reading this will pursue this matter further.[126] It seems that some see the immediate connection between one's views of hermeneutics, the kingdom and eschatology and how they relate to the missionary task,[127] but it seems that few conservative Evangelicals and Fundamentalists have seen the need to pursue the matter theologically and explain it for the benefit of the Church. Consider these words:

"Theological studies that link missions to contemporary biblical research in hermeneutics, the kingdom of God, eschatology and church/world relations are relatively infrequent and unsophisticated."[128]

My words here are among the "unsophisticated." May God use someone reading this to show God's people how such matters are directly connected to our understanding of the Great Commission.

When we add to the Great Commission the burden of solving world poverty and social ills, the Great Commission becomes distorted. So does the job description of the preacher of the Gospel. On the practical level, the Great

---

125 McCune, Rolland. (2004). *Promise Unfulfilled: The Failed Strategy of Modern Evangelicalism,* p. 265. Greenville, SC: Ambassador Emerald International. McCune tackles the issue of social action at some length in this book from a Dispensational Baptist perspective.

126 Ronald E. Diprose shows the origin, spread, and impact of replacement theology throughout Church history in his book *Israel and the Church: The Origins and Effects of Replacement Theology* (Authentic Media, 2000).

127 I have only been able to find brief treatments of these topics, such as blog posts. Jesse Johnson has some thought-provoking blog posts on *Cripplegate* (*http://thecripplegate.com*) such as "Discontinuity: the poor, Israel, and the Church" (Sept. 20, 2011) and "Dispensationalism, Keller, and the Poor" (Aug. 16, 2011).

128 D. G. Reid, R. D. Linder, B. L. Shelley, and H. S. Stout. (1990). *Dictionary of Christianity in America.* Downers Grove, IL: InterVarsity Press. Found in the article entitled "Protestant Missiology."

Commission is *simple; all* believers in *every* place and in *all* circumstances can fulfill this command and imitate the example given to us in the New Testament.

Every earnest missionary must tackle this issue of the kingdom and what it means or does not mean for them as individual laborers. If not, confusion will continue to reign, and virtually all methods for missions will be deemed good and acceptable, even equal, in fulfilling the Great Commission.[129] For me, preaching the kingdom of God means declaring the message of sal-

---

> *"... the Great Commission is simple; all believers in every place and in all circumstances can fulfill this command ..."*

---

vation so that those who are in darkness may come to the light, that those in the kingdom of Satan be delivered through the cross, entering God's spiritual kingdom which will one day be made visible.[130] As God blesses my attempts to make disciples in His name, it is my task to teach those new believers what it means to be salt and light in their communities,[131] showing what transformed life in Christ looks like to those around them. As more and more experience eternal life, the influence of the Gospel will increase on the societal level, impacting it for righteousness. All institutional attempts to extend kingdom influence apart from Gospel proclamation and discipleship are illegitimate.

---

129 David Hesselgrave attempts to raise the importance of these and other issues and how they influence missionary methods in his book *Paradigms in Conflict: 10 Key Questions in Missions Today* (Kregel, 2006).

130 Acts 26:18; 1 John 3:8; 5:18–20.

131 Matt. 5:1–16

Who Is Our Paradigm for Cross-Cultural Missions, Jesus or Paul?

Some brethren seek to promote the global social work agenda by turning to Jesus as their paradigm. Is it legitimate to use Jesus and the accounts of His ministry as exemplary of cross-cultural missionary methodology for the Church? We must consider this matter carefully.

It is important that we consider the serious limits that are inherent in using the Lord Himself as our example for Gospel ministry. He was the incarnate Son of God, the Messiah, whose task was to fulfill Old Testament prophecy and the law and to give His life as a ransom for many. The Church of the new covenant did not yet exist, nor had the Great Commission been given when He and His disciples walked throughout Judea, an area He rarely left. In His earthly ministry He was homeless, travelled with a large number of disciples, and spent much time in the temple and in Jewish synagogues. He worked miracles of incredible proportion, taught in parables and mysteries, and ministered almost solely to the Jews. After His death, burial, and resurrection, Jesus gave His disciples, those who would lay the foundation of His Church, the Great Commission before ascending into heaven.

After the Holy Spirit was given to God's people in Acts 2, we saw throughout Acts to Revelation what the fulfillment of the Great Commission meant. This makes the ministry of the apostles, and primarily that of Paul as the missionary to the Gentiles, our primary example for cross-cultural ministry.[132] While the apostles did miracles at times and exercised spiritual gifts no longer in use today, their ministries did not revolve around these activities. We are not even given the impression that these were a normal part of their ministries. Paul was conscious of the fact that he exemplified

---

132   Eckhard Schnabel's work *Paul the Missionary: Realities, Strategies, and Methods* (InterVarsity Press, 2009) is a thorough treatment of Paul's life as missionary to the Gentiles. He seeks to make applications of Paul's example for believers pursuing the fulfillment of the Great Commission today.

Jesus Christ in the context of cross-cultural missions. This is why he could so boldly ask God's people to imitate him.[133]

Those who reason that Jesus is our primary example for how to fulfill the Great Commission see little value in considering the teaching and model of the apostles in regards to that mission. In their minds Jesus' example is far more important and binding. In a discussion about why it is that Christians ignore Paul's apostolic methods a believer once said to me, "Because we are obeying Jesus, not Paul." These words convey a tension between the example of Jesus and that of Paul and the apostles.

We must not allow ourselves to think that there is a spiritual conflict between what Jesus did in His earthly ministry and what Paul exemplified for us. The ministry of Jesus and the ministry of Paul were accomplishing different things. Paul was commissioned by Christ, enabled and led by His Holy Spirit as a Gospel foundation builder for His Gentile church. He obeyed Jesus' teachings but his ministry was much different than that of Jesus. Was he rebelling against God's paradigm of kingdom ministry? Were he and all of the other apostles and apostolic co-laborers just ignorant of Jesus' methods? No, these men and women were exemplifying for the church what it meant to obey Jesus Christ and fulfill the Great Commission. There were no inconsistencies between their methods and Christ's teachings.

If a Cambodian Christian were to pick up his Bible and look for instruction on how to fulfill the Great Commission, he would not look to the Old Testament or to the ministry of Jesus—unless a foreigner instructs him to do so. He will naturally look to the apostles. So should we.

David Hesselgrave encourages us to revisit the arguments that Roland Allen set forth years ago for using the Apostle Paul as the paradigm for world missions:

> "Before concluding, I think it prudent to repeat and reinforce Allen's basic thesis yet once more. Paul is the divinely appointed model for missionaries of succeeding generations. This thesis was by no means original to Allen, of course ... . Then, when writing the pref-

---

133   1 Cor. 4:16; 11:1; Phil. 3:17

ace to the second edition of Missionary Methods, Allen reviewed both what he had written in the first edition and how it had been received, concluding, 'I myself am more convinced than ever that in the careful examination of his [Paul's] work, above all in the understanding and appreciation of his principles, we shall find the solution of most of our present difficulties.'"[134]

I believe, as Allen, that many of the problems faced by missionaries and those seeking to promote Christ around the world would be put behind them if only they would resubmit themselves to New Testament priorities and principles regarding the fulfillment of the Great Commission.[135]

A Closer Look at Poverty: What Is It? What Is the Church to Do about It?

There are thousands of foreigners in Cambodia who have devoted themselves to solving or relieving poverty through the following kinds of activities:

- building school buildings, funding public school teacher salaries, sponsoring students, providing school lunches for students
- digging wells and fish ponds in villages, micro-financing for farmers and small businesses
- educating the people about sanitation, basic health, sexual diseases, and women empowerment
- seeking to impact the culture of domestic violence by advocating for human rights
- teaching English, computer skills, cooking, and other job-related skills
- promoting Cambodian arts and crafts

---

134   Robert L. Plummer and John Mark Terry. (2012). *Paul's Missionary Methods: In His Time and Ours* (Kindle Locations 1468–1470). Downers Grove, IL: IVP Academic.

135   A thorough treatment on the importance of the Apostle Paul as the paradigm for the missions in the Church today is Christopher Little's *Mission in the Way of Paul: Biblical Mission for the Church in the Twenty-First Century* (Peter Lang, 2005).

- helping government agencies develop in technology
- supporting orphanages, feeding centers, and medical clinics
- facilitating scholarships for education abroad, teaching modern farming technology, teaching sports

The list can go on.

Aid agencies and their impact surround us daily. There are over forty aid agencies with a continual presence in Pursat province, with many more agencies that come and go.

The list above contains many good deeds and worthy causes, numerous activities that encourage better living and more social and economic development. Some of these are done alongside active Christian witness or even as an integral part of church planting strategies. No Christian would dare say that such activities are wrong in themselves!

My question, however, is this: when the Bible speaks of the poor, what kind of person is being referred to? When we as individuals are called upon to help the weak, who is in view? I believe that many Christians today do not understand what genuine poverty is. As a result many confuse development projects and social betterment, which make up a large portion of social action, with the kind of poverty relief described in the Scriptures.

Simply put, in Scripture the poor are those that have no food, no clothing, or no shelter. The poor are those with nothing; they have no one to depend upon and are unable to survive apart from emergency aid given by others. Shocked? Study the Scriptures to arrive at a clear definition.

In the book of Job we find a very wealthy man known for his faith and active righteousness. His wealth and status was so great that he was not much different from a king in many ways. We find him later devastated by trials and sufferings inflicted upon him by Satan by the permission of God. Much of the book includes Job's despair and confusion about why God would allow all of this to happen to him, for he knows all things are in God's direct control. In the book, Job feels that injustice is being done to him, so he seeks to prove his righteousness. As Job describes his life as a wealthy rich man whose ways please God, we find that he speaks much about his treatment of the poor. His words help us define who the poor really are.[136] We also must remember that Job was able to do what he did because of his incredible wealth, wealth that very few believers reading this today possess.

When Jesus speaks about trusting God for our daily needs, He is careful to mention only food and clothing.[137] Beloved Tabitha, who was raised from the dead by Peter, was known throughout the city of Joppa for her provision of clothing for widows.[138] When James states the necessity of caring for

---

"... the poor are those who have no food, clothing, or shelter."

---

orphans and widows, he is talking about this kind of emergency aid.[139] The apostle John describes genuine love among brethren as not allowing others in our fellowship to suffer destitution or need such as this without aid. Believers in Jesus Christ must respond to such needs that are around them. The love of God demands it.[140] Paul told Timothy to teach that food and raiment was enough for people to be content, a definition that must inform how we define genuine poverty.[141] Widows were not allowed to be added to the list for regular assistance unless they had no family to help them.[142]

We can conclude, then, that the poor are those who have no food, clothing, or shelter. They are also completely dependent upon the mercy of others for their survival. Depending on the culture, widows, orphans, and the physically handicapped can be especially vulnerable to this state of poverty.

---

136   Job 24:1–11; 29:12–16; 31:16–22

137   Matt. 6:25–34

138   Acts 9:36–43

139   Jam. 1:27

140   1 John 3:16–18

141   1 Tim. 6:8

142   1 Tim. 5:3–16

Many people talking about helping the poor today are not referring to the destitute—those who have no food or clothing and nowhere to turn because of extreme circumstances. Instead, much time, energy, and resources are spent on improving the quality of life and increasing wealth among others that have these basic needs met but have less than ourselves. Many of these attempts are aimed at trying to force secular and pagan governments to live according to a misunderstanding of God's laws to the theocracy of Israel. What the Scripture demands of the Church in this age is much different.[143]

If our churches indeed have excess wealth and none around us are in need, we certainly have the freedom and privilege of giving to meet the needs of poverty in faraway places. This is easier to do now than ever before in world history. However, decisions about what we actually do with those funds need to be carefully made and biblically informed.

What kinds of aid fall into the biblical definition of real need? Emergency aid in refugee camps, famine relief, orphanages in places ravaged by epidemics or war, and assistance in times of extreme natural disasters where people are unable to help themselves—these are the kinds of poverty relief and aid work that should be top priority. So many of the other activities championed as poverty relief and social action today are actually addressing relative wealth, not the issue of genuine poverty.[144]

---

143   A missionary who seemed to understand these dynamics well is John L. Nevius, missionary to China in the nineteenth century. His biography gives illustrations of what kinds of relief he did in his ministry. *The Life of John Livingston Nevius: For Forty Years a Missionary in China* was written by his wife, Helen (Fleming H. Revell, 1895). This book is available for free in digital formats. A book covering his discourses on methodology is also helpful for showing how Nevius thought through these issues: The Planting and Development of Missionary Churches (Monadnock Press, 2003). Originally published in 1895, this book is a compilation of addresses given to new missionaries who had just arrived in Korea. God greatly used these addresses in the lives of these missionaries.

144   Some might ask about the gifts to the church in Jerusalem. The only example we have in the NT of one church helping another church body financially was the famine relief for the Jerusalem church (Acts 11:27–30; 15:1–29; 1 Cor. 16:1–3; 2 Cor. 8–9; Gal 2). These gifts were indeed motivated by compassion because of persecution and natural disaster, but they were primarily motivated by the need to express unity in the body of Christ because of great theological tension. The Gentiles needed to prove their oneness with the Jews who struggled with their inclusion in the church, the body of Christ. They also needed to

God's people in every culture and circumstance can reach out to those around them who are poor as defined here. The only ones who cannot are those in these very extreme circumstances themselves. National local churches are required to show the love of Christ and to help the poor that are around them—the poor as defined by the Scriptures, not the relatively poor as compared to more affluent societies.

As a missionary in Cambodia, I see relative poverty daily. I see people living in tiny cheap wood shacks with tin roofs alongside huge and unbelievably expensive villas. I see people who possess only one bicycle for their entire family's transportation while other families have multiple cars and motorcycles with fewer people to drive them. Some people strive with all of their being to put food on the table and pay for their children's minimal education, while others have so much money they do not even know what to do with it. Some are illiterate and ignorant of the wider world outside their own community while others are highly educated and surf the internet all day long on their new iPad! One family might have no money to purchase electricity, not even owning a car battery from which to power a light, while another family lights up an entire complex all night long without even flinching at the cost.

What is my responsibility to those with less? As a preacher of the Gospel, or even as a Christian, is it my role to seek to help them catch up to those with more? My duty is to preach Christ to them! What is my responsibility to those with more? Confront them with the Gospel—the same responsibility that my Cambodian brethren have—and no more. It is the poor in spirit, those who mourn over sin, that we can truly help.[145] These are those we seek to minister to.

We have observed that many middle to upper-middle class people are interested in sending money abroad for aid work. These believers are often geographically and socially secluded from those who are categorized low-income or impoverished in their own culture. Some may not even believe that there are any real poor in America because of government aid. Their lives are

---

express gratitude for being used of God to bring the Gospel to them. These gifts were not continual.

145 Matt. 5:3–4

so isolated from the poor that they have no experience with helping those in great need. At the same time, they feel guilty that their lives are lived so easily compared to many in the world and they want to do something. The answer for many to relieve their conscience is to write checks for charity work overseas. We suggest that these believers refrain from sending money overseas until they have spent much time in helping those in their own city or county first. Experiences gained from this will give them much practical wisdom in applying the Scriptures and will keep them from pursuing the wild idealism that is promoted by many of the aid agencies competing for their contributions. They will find that they are much more careful in decisions to send money abroad.

Some missionaries working in relatively poor cultures get frustrated with the lack of resources within the national churches. They see that most of those who come to Christ are not the movers and shakers of society. This does not fit within the missionary's ambition to have thriving churches with lots of money for programs and institutions. They want the local church to support its pastor full-time and to send out missionaries. They need money! Some missionaries then conclude that their role is to provide job skills and professional training to converts so that they can make more money and thus, it is supposed, support the ministry for which the missionary envisions. Does the New Testament justify such a strategy? What is communicated to the national church through such methods? To me this causes problems on a number of fronts, which I think this book already addresses in different ways, but will become clearer in Factor number 7.

Now that we have discussed how theology impacts one's view of the Great Commission and the missionary task, we will consider more about how our understanding of poverty impacts our methodology.

Challenges and Blessings to Pioneer Missions

Challenges:

False Christianity and the cults aggressively use caring for physical needs as leverage for gaining converts. Converts come much more quickly when they are purchased. The tension between showing the love of Christ through good works and the avoidance of patronage is a constant burden.

When national believers meet Bible-believing missionaries whose methodology radically differs from one another, it causes confusion. There can even be tension between good missionaries because of these differences. Those who seek to follow closely to New Testament example are often misunderstood by those who have been taught an entirely different paradigm for missions. Missionaries burdened about the need for God's people to recover New Testament methods in missions practice often find it difficult to avoid a critical and judgmental spirit toward those that differ and vice versa.

Blessings:

Working among the relatively poor keeps us focused on eternal things as opposed to the temporal. It is a blessing to see relatively poor believers learn to live out their faith in their own culture without the burdens churches in the West have placed upon themselves because of materialism. As we watch them, we see that they enjoy God's promises fulfilled toward them just as much in their context as we do in our own context back home.

Factor 7:
A consistently spiritual focus of ministry can be difficult to maintain.

Keeping the Gospel Clear Among the Poor

Missionaries serving in places where relative poverty is the norm (most of the world!) need to preach the Gospel carefully in order to avoid communicating that Christianity provides hope for financial security, a hope on earth. Unbelievers will be tempted to adjust the Gospel into a prosperity gospel, because that is the kind of gospel an unregenerate man wants—a new and more effective version of the false religion he already possesses. Some are willing to worship any god that might potentially help them out of their difficulties. Others try adding Jesus to their gods in order to see if doing so will help them financially. Scripture tells us that false teachers will exploit this very desire and thrive.[146] And so they do, all over the world today.

The Gospel laborer must have a thorough understanding of what the Word of God promises, as well as what it does not promise in regard to the poor and oppressed.[147] The commission that Jesus gave Paul was to preach the Gospel to the nations in order that they be delivered from Satan and enter into God's kingdom, so they might receive forgiveness of sins and obtain an eternal inheritance in Him. Those that desire this salvation must repent and have lives that reflect that repentance by the grace of God.[148] Peter at Pentecost set forth the immediate reward of repentance and faith as being

---

146   1 Tim. 6:3–5; 2 Tim. 4:3–4; 2 Pet. 2:1–3

147   While the Gospel does indeed have a great impact upon our life in the here and now, our hope is not to be placed in this life or in this world dominated by sin, death, and the curse. Our hope is to be placed in Christ's coming, the resurrection, His reign, and the new heaven and new earth (1 Cor. 15; 2 Pet. 3:1–13; Rev. 20–22).

148   Acts 26:16–20

forgiveness of sins and the gift of the Holy Spirit as the down payment of the eternal inheritance.[149]

When we first came to Cambodia, the nation was just beginning to come out of several long, painful, and dark decades of war and intense poverty. Many had experienced the compassion of foreign aid organizations and relief organizations, many of them Christian, whether within Cambodia's borders or in the refugee camps in Thailand. As the country opened up for religious freedom and foreign missionaries began to arrive in the 1990s, most of them preached the Gospel while also providing services: free English lessons, training in job skills, feeding centers, orphanages, food pantries, and even monthly stipends to faithful members. The result of this was the Cambodian view that Christianity was either for people who were desperately poor and needed to beg to survive, or for those who had an entrepreneurial spirit and were willing to convert to a foreign religion to climb out of poverty. Because of this, when we witnessed for Christ, an immediate question was, "What will you give me if I become a Christian?" A second question also asked was, "If I go to your church, do you have any positions available for work?"

Cambodia was in desperate need for immediate relief aid after Pol Pot and the Khmer Rouge.[150] Praise God for Christians that gave and labored in compassion at that time, especially in the refugee camps. Many lives were spared and the love of Christ was shown to the Cambodian people. However, after the nation began to climb out of its extreme circumstances, the aid agencies and compassion ministries did not leave. Instead they radically multiplied, so much so that Cambodia is one of the most "aid-agencied" countries in the world.[151] Most Christian workers still combine social work with church-planting efforts. And many who profess Christ for financial gain or educational benefits revert to Folk Buddhism after they have ex-

---

149   Acts 2:37–39

150   If you are unaware of Cambodia's turbulent twentieth century, especially the 1970s, I encourage you to simply "google" the Khmer Rouge and it will not take you long to find plenty of information on this tragic time of the nation's history.

151   According to World Bank, 12.5 percent of Cambodia's GDP was foreign aid! Cambodia is ranked number twenty-four of the world's top twenty-five aid-receiving nations (*http://www.statisticbrain.com/countries-with-highest-foreign-aid-statistics/*).

hausted whatever aid was obtainable. Many who continue in Christianity through these venues distort the message of the Gospel into a prosperity gospel.

I have been greatly disappointed as I have seen so many well-meaning brothers and sisters fall into the same trap that has menaced missions in recent history, encouraging "rice Christianity" by coupling charity with evangelism. The term "rice Christians" refers to those who profess faith in Jesus Christ and are motivated by a desire for some material gain—rice, for example. Various mission agencies report of revivals and multitudes coming to Christ because believers dug wells. Another may tell of many children professing faith in Jesus after being fed at centers.

Around the time of this writing, I interviewed eight small church fellowships in the province of Oddar Meanchey. I discovered that several of the churches were born not too long after the refugee camps were closed in the mid-1990s. Some of their leaders were converts from the camps. Early on, each church had quite a large group of people meeting together (scores of people—quite large for Cambodia), most of whom professed Christ in the refugee camps during evangelistic crusades held in conjunction with aid efforts there, or soon thereafter. As several years passed and foreign aid became more irregular, most of the professed believers in these churches fell away. Some will still come to church today, but only when a foreigner shows up with rice or medicine. Now, between two and fifteen members meet in each of these fellowships. In conversation, each church leader has laid blame on the handouts scheme of evangelism used by Christian aid organizations to secure converts while also relieving poverty.

The churches here are in a state of depression. Knowing all of the problems the foreign aid has caused, some of them still allow foreigners to come into their assemblies and give their handouts and "preach the good news." Evangelism for them in the past has largely revolved around these special meetings with handouts, which has proved devastating to biblical discipleship. The churches have not learned to preach the Gospel and see God's Spirit convert sinners through normal life and relationships.

And how does the unbelieving community looking on respond to this? They scorn Christianity as they see fellow villagers falsely profess and show up for handouts, only to return to their sin after they obtained their share. This shames the faithful believers even further, silencing their witness. This also confirms to the financially self-sufficient locals that the Gospel is only for the desperate who need handouts, hardening them in their pride against

---

"God's people back home allow their emotions and hunger for optimistic reports to sweep away their theology and their life experience in evangelism when it comes to what happens on the mission field."

---

the Gospel message. Who is ultimately to blame for this deplorable state of affairs? Not the Cambodians! Instead, it is the often well-intentioned foreign Christian donors who have been told that believers must feed the body before they can feed the soul. They have been persuaded that missions must be "holistic," meeting the physical needs of a person so that you can minister to their spiritual need.

God's people back home allow their emotions and hunger for optimistic reports to sweep away their theology and their life experience in evangelism when it comes to what happens on the mission field. Missionaries on the ground who know the language and the culture where these things are supposedly taking place grieve at the naiveté of those that support such things. It seems like more and more of God's people back home in sending countries, who would never have fallen for such diversions from sound theology and practice in the past, are caving in to such appeals and reports at an alarming rate. As technology has greatly improved, emotionally charged professionally filmed presentations with well-written scripts that encourage unbiblical ideas of missions have become more influential. These powerfully persuasive appeals disarm the discernment of many good people.

Cambodia has a proverb: "Grow rice with water; wage war with rice."[152] Those in secular power know that wielding food and comfort is the most powerful weapon in achieving political will over any people. In religious proselytizing, this is also the most "effective" method where relative poverty is the norm. For this reason, the false religions and cults here in Cambodia aggressively use money to buy converts outright. Why do they do this? That's simple: wage war with rice. Bible-believing Christians should never stoop to such faithless and degrading methods! And yet for many Christian groups, there is no distinction between their methods and that of these false religions.[153] Some would even argue that the Gospel message has no power apart from such manipulation of the lost! They suggest, "People can't hear the Gospel on empty stomachs." Here is one response to this thinking:

> "The belief that the natural man with an empty belly cannot respond to the call for repentance and faith is strange theology indeed. It is Arminian, if not Pelagian, in content: it assumes that one's stomach ultimately controls his response to the gospel, or else it presupposes some form of volitional equilibrium by which a person has no inclination for or against the gospel except through their glands. This is not only unscriptural, it is inherently unstable and self-destructive because it has no limiting notion … . Such an approach is an insult to God's sovereign grace and unlimited power to save whom He will by the means He has clearly established."[154]

---

152   Fressanges, Alain. (2010). *Khmer Sayings*, p. 86. Phnom Penh: KCD Publishing.

153   In Cambodia, the Roman Catholic Church, Jehovah's Witnesses, and Mormons are all well-known for this approach to proselytizing. Even radical Muslims from the Middle East are using this approach among the large Cham Muslim minority in hopes of one day radicalizing them.

154   McCune, Rolland. (2004). *Promise Unfulfilled*, p. 273. Ambassador Emerald International.

The Local Church: Guarding Spiritual Relationships Amid Relative Poverty

Foreign missionaries must express Christ-likeness through giving while avoiding the trap of the patron-client dynamic which the world uses for power and influence. Missionaries must not allow themselves to be perceived as "the Great White Missionary."[155] Financial dependence upon the missionary results in the patron-client relationship.

What are patron-client relationships? Patron-client relationships refer to a relationship where one person is financially dependent upon another. Usually faithfulness or loyalty is given by the one who receives compensation for the generosity shown by the patron. This is a normal aspect of life in many cultures and is not in itself wrong. Those who create financial dependence in the name of missions among peoples in such cultures (which includes most of the world) will always fall into the patron role or this relationship, regardless of their intentions to the contrary.

In Christ's Body, however, the Bible gives no room for a spiritual leader to be the financial patron of those he ministers to. The spiritual leader, if anything, is to be either dependent upon the congregation he serves[156] or follow Paul's example and be independent for strategic ministry reasons.[157]

When the missionary becomes a financial patron for those to whom he is ministering, he fails to guard the vital spiritual relationship between himself and the national believers. His authority and leadership become derived from his money and its power, rather than from the things of the Spirit.

It is very significant that the apostles and their co-laborers are never seen in the New Testament as patrons in any other way than patrons on the spiritual level. The local churches were dependent upon the apostolic laborers for

---

155 Or "Great Filipino, Korean, Brazilian, or any other ethnic background Missionary."

156 1 Cor. 9:1–14; Gal. 6:6; 1 Tim. 5:17–18

157 1 Cor. 9:1–27; 1 Thess. 2:9; 2 Thess. 3:6–15

spiritual ministry alone: the teaching of the Word of God, counsel, accountability, and encouragement.

Jean Johnson asks some penetrating questions:

> "It is possible that those who do missions from North America may have lost the ability to plant the gospel in other nations without setting ourselves up in a patron-client relationship. We use our expertise, services, and money to put ourselves in a position where people need us, and then we share the gospel from that patron platform. But in the long run, is patron-client evangelism reproducible for those who emulate us? Can they constantly bring the gospel to their cities and villages by providing goods and services? Furthermore, is this approach even biblical? Was Paul tossed out of so many places because he made himself needed by the people he ministered to? Why was the apostle Paul driven— often violently— from so many cities and towns? Did he not know about the patron-client method of church planting?"[158]

Many pioneer missionaries feel a constant tension between the twin necessities of being full of good works and that of avoiding financial patronage. In Cambodia we have prayed for and sought opportunities to show the love of Christ in appropriate ways that would not hurt our spiritual relationships. We have taken in an unbelieving orphan for several months. We have assisted people with medical needs or basic daily staples—I delivered a small box of food items and medicine just this morning to a man who asked to borrow money from me. We have contributed to various projects in the areas we minister in, such as small road projects or gifts to the public school. These are all private gifts, irregular expressions of love which do not create dependence or distort our spiritual relationships. Avoiding dependence does not necessarily mean that we must fail to be compassionate or generous.

Sometimes national believers see the need to avoid a financial patron-client relationship with the missionary. Patronage of national believers does not only affect the missionary's testimony, but also that of the national believers.

---

158 Johnson, Jean. (2012, 16 October). *We Are Not the Hero* (Kindle Locations 5266–5272). Deep River Books. Kindle Edition.

Hooie, a young woman who came to Christ, experienced great persecution. At the time of her conversion she was working for us as house help. She concluded that working for us was hurting her testimony because people claimed that her profession to faith in Christ was linked to working for us. In other words, they said that she was converting for financial gain. Hooie quit working for us in order to silence this slander.

Another time, the church in Pursat, which meets in a larger home of one of the members, was in need of a wall around its property in order to guard its property lines. We offered to help with the cost of the building project, only to be rebuffed by the homeowner who wanted to promote the independence of the church from foreign influence. It was very important for them to be able to tell the unsaved world around them that the wall was built from their own funds. Therefore they turned away financial assistance.

A great distortion of spiritual relationships has occurred within the churches of Cambodia that has greatly weakened its Gospel foundation. As we read Acts and the Epistles, we see that church-planting missionaries are to be laborers of the Gospel, deriving their authority and influence within the Church from the ministry of the Word alone. But in many places Gospel workers derive their authority and influence within the Church from their ability to obtain and wield funds from abroad. It is a great privilege to be able to stand with national believers as spiritual equals without the burden of the patron-client relationship and its effects. Many missionaries never know this privilege.[159]

---

159   A missionary biography that provides a great help for what pioneer church planting among the relatively poor should look like is Geraldine Taylor's *Behind the Ranges: The Life-Changing Story of J.O. Fraser* (OMF Books, 1998). Many of the thoughts communicated in this book are reflected in the life and ministry of J.O. Fraser. He understood the necessity of maintaining these important relationship dynamics.

The Local Church: National Leadership in the Midst of Relative Poverty

Many good missionary brethren have a blind spot when it comes to the realities and dangers of the patron-client relationship. They simply do not understand that the way they use their money affects not only their own relationship with national believers, but also relationships between the nationals themselves.

Many good national brethren see the dangers and greatly regret the damage done through them, but they do not face up to the reality and cut themselves off from it. Why? Many are already dependent and see no way out. Some enjoy the raised social status and material lift provided through the

---

"... spiritual leadership as depicted in the New Testament functions exactly opposite that of the patron-client leadership structure of the world."

---

patronage from abroad and know that when the money ends, so does their raised status and lifestyle. Others think that they can somehow be an exception and turn the situation around, but I have met none who have succeeded.

Leadership in patron-client cultures is achieved by power, prestige, money, and family ties. Leadership is sustained by maintaining loyalty of followers through material benefits and by flexing political muscle. When the missionary leads churches from the position of a financial patron, even if he does so in love and meekness, he communicates to the national church that leadership in the local church mirrors that of the world. This is a tragedy, because spiritual leadership as depicted in the New Testament functions exactly opposite that of the patron-client leadership structure of the world.[160] New Testament local-church leadership has nothing to do with

---

160 Matt. 20:25–28

money, prestige, political influence, status in society, etc., but everything to do with all things spiritual. Leaders are to obtain their position of authority and influence within the Church because of their character, spiritual gifts, and knowledge of God and His Word—that is all. Their ministry is to teach and shepherd, encourage and rebuke, and watch over the souls of their flock.

There is a far better relationship intended by God between the spiritual leader and those he leads to Christ. It is much deeper than the patron-client relationship, and it is limited to the spiritual level. This relationship is described in the New Testament as spiritual parenting. The apostles exemplify this for us.[161]

Many Cambodian pastors have greatly suffered in their ministries because of this unbiblical view of leadership. Already their society's tendency is to default to the material patron-client style of leadership. When foreign missionaries come in wielding their large ministry budgets, this is perceived by the nationals as typical wielding of power and influence found in their native culture. Then they assume that Christian leadership must be just a sanctified version of the patron-client relationships around them.

To many national pastors, the only model of leadership they have ever seen is the financial/political patron-client relationship. The missionary laying the foundation of the Gospel is supposed to be teaching them to follow the New Testament pattern—which is the opposite of that material patron-client system. If the missionary himself models a financial patron-client leadership style, the national pastors themselves will likely never arrive at biblical spiritual leadership on their own. Missionaries cannot expect the national pastors to function under a leadership model that the missionaries themselves did not teach or emulate.

---

161 John clearly held this relationship with those he ministered to. He refers to them as his children, reminding them of this relationship (1 John 2:1, 18, 28; 5:21; 3Jn 4). Paul emphasizes this spiritual parenting relationship as well (1 Cor. 4:14–21); the entire book of 2 Corinthians is filled with allusions to this relationship between Paul and the Corinthian believers. The theme can also be traced in terms of honor and shame throughout the book. A thorough study of the epistles would reveal this spiritual version of the patron-client in many other passages as well.

In our ministry we teach the local church's responsibility of giving to its spiritual leadership from the beginning. We make it clear that national pastors must be cared for by God's people to whom they minister.[162] As temporary cross-cultural missionaries, we forego our right to this kind of support from those to whom we minister, even as did Paul.[163] We do, however, often accept remuneration through various love gifts, such as modest gifts of food, travel funds, etc. Why should we accept these? Because the New Testament clearly teaches a mutual reciprocity: those who minister to God's people spiritually must themselves be ministered to materially. In this God is glorified because His people are showing love, honor and gratitude toward those who teach and lead them in His truth.

We also believe that the support of national pastors with foreign funds, even when a foreign missionary is not present, is spiritually dangerous. God clearly commands His people to support their spiritual leaders. When national churches do not support their own spiritual leadership because this responsibility is being met by believers in other places, the reciprocal ministry dynamic mentioned above does not take place. This results in a distorted relationship dynamic within the assembly. God in His wisdom ordained that local churches support their pastors in order to maintain healthy spiritual relationships. To choose another paradigm for supporting pastors, regardless of the ministry strategy objectives, is at the least dangerous.[164]

---

162   1 Cor. 9:1–18; Gal.6:6; 1 Tim. 5:17–18

163   There are various reasons why the apostle Paul did not accept remuneration when he was bringing the Gospel as a pioneer missionary, including: not wanting to be identified with the traveling religious teachers and philosophers of his day (a theme throughout 1 Corinthians); to avoid being perceived as preaching the Gospel out of greed (1 Thess. 2:1–8); to avoid being a burden to the young churches (1 Thess. 2:9); as a tentmaker he sought to be an example of Christian work ethic for those struggling with laziness (2 Thess. 3:6–15).

164   In the previously referenced book, *Mission in the Way of Paul*, Christopher Little argues biblically and thoroughly against the practice of what is commonly referred to as "International Partnership Missions." The IPM movement, which can be simply described as sending money to support churches, leaders, and their ministries in foreign countries, has had a devastating effect upon the Church worldwide, and the practice only continues to grow.

God's people may not be able to support their pastor full-time, but they must support him according to their ability. In this way they show obedience to Christ. By this they also show their honor and gratitude for their pastor's labor of love.[165]

As we consider the issues regarding national leadership and our relationship to them, we must remember this important point: as cross-cultural laborers for the Gospel, we must discipline our minds and hearts to consistently look at all of these issues through the eyes of the people in the culture where we are laboring, not through the lens of our own cultural perspective.

Pastor Ti in Pursat understands the issues involved. He is an electrician by trade. He repairs electronics and appliances and his family does others things as well to help make ends meet. The small church gives him a salary—one that is woefully inadequate to support his family—but it is according to their means. The people regularly bring him love gifts: fish caught in the river or rice paddies; fruit and vegetables from members' gardens; sacks of rice from their harvest yields, etc. In this way they obey the Lord Jesus Christ and the spiritual relationship dynamic exemplified in the New Testament is worked out to God's glory.

From a "strategic" and pragmatic business perspective, it would be much easier to find funds from overseas and support local pastors full-time. As strategic as this funding might seem in providing quick results, ultimately a decision to do this results in a failure in discipleship in the life of the newly founded church. It seems that many of God's people have unwittingly allowed the philosophy of the secular business world to dominate their thinking to the point that they elevate principles of "good business" above the Scriptures. God's ways simply do not fit within the collective wisdom of even the best of secular business models. God's wisdom will always be folly to the world.[166]

---

165   If you would like to pursue this matter further, consider an article that we have written with Chris Seawright that was published in the Ohio Bible Fellowship's newsletter, The Visitor (June-July 2007) entitled "Stewardship in Foreign Missions: Should Foreigners Support National Leaders?" It can be found at *http://obfvisitor.wordpress.com/2007/06/01/ stewardship-in-foreign-missions-part 1/#more-61.*

166   1 Cor. 1:18–2:16

How does foreign funding of pastors and churches impact the national church practically? The people learn to turn to the foreign missionary to meet their needs, provide for them in time of crisis, provide buildings, and insure aid from abroad. When a national pastor takes over for the missionary, the mold has already been cast—the national pastor now must be the one who takes care of the financial needs of the assembly and finds ways to obtain money from foreign sources. They are saddled with burdens that they are not supposed to bear, burdens that were not theirs to begin with.

As a result, many Cambodian pastors are reduced to being frustrated patrons rather than spiritual leaders. They are frustrated because they do not have the financial ability to maintain the patron-client leadership role. Their members are frustrated too, because they expect their pastors to come through and take care of their physical needs, but they cannot. And national pastors who are able to find the funds get sucked into the downward spiral of dependency which is yet another handicap.

As pioneer missionaries work out how to live with compassion amidst relative poverty, they must be focused on keeping the Gospel clear, guarding their spiritual relationships, fervently meeting spiritual needs, while keeping ministry methods reproducible. Then the relatively poor local church will be empowered, the foundation of the Gospel will be faithfully laid, national men will easily be able to assume leadership, and the churches will see that fulfilling the Great Commission is within their reach.[167]

Some might be wishing that I would be more practical and provide some down-to-earth examples of how foreign missionaries might give and still avoid the trap of the patron-client relationships. I will attempt to answer this here. A philosophy of missionary giving that is consistent with what is expressed in this book should look something like this:

1. While we are grieved by numerous social ills and relative poverty all around us, we do not bear the burden of responsibility to solve these problems. Our desire is to preach the Gospel, delivering peo-

---

167 Consider reading my unpublished article, "Should We Support National Leaders? A Plea from a Missionary," found here: *http://media.sermonaudio.com/articles/fo-531116130-1.pdf*.

ple from the power of Satan and unto God so that they might receive an eternal inheritance in Jesus Christ.

2. We are responsible to exemplify what it means to be a godly Christian to those around us by being generous according to our means as a family.

3. We are responsible to respond to instances of emergency needs that we are made aware of within our sphere of influence according to our means as exemplified in the parable of the Good Samaritan.

4. When we give, we need to do so according to our status within the community. As foreigners, we need to give more than the average Cambodian would, but not beyond reason (in their view) to avoid appearing like one trying to become a patron.

5. We must remember that when material needs are brought to the attention of the local church, it is the responsibility of that local church to act. In the community of believers each responds according to his/her individual ability. The missionaries represent just one family among many who need to respond biblically in a crisis.

6. When we are burdened to give financial assistance, we must seek Cambodian counsel about how best to help and not trust our limited foreign judgment.

7. When we are asked for a personal loan, it is better to give a gift rather than enter into a financially obligatory relationship. This keeps those appealing for aid from unnecessary shame and guards against losing relationships with those unable to repay loans.[168]

8. We have decided to never give beggar children money so as to not encourage the exploitation of children by traffickers. If we give to children, it must be something that will help the child only, like food (and maybe even something that cannot be resold for money!).

9. Other than small money gifts which are acceptable in this culture for the destitute, we do not give money to people who ask for fi-

---

168 Dr. John Dreisbach, long-time medical missionary who labored in many countries, was on the leadership of our mission toward the end of his life. He visited us in Cambodia early in our ministry. One point he stressed to us was the necessity to avoid the giving of personal loans, especially to those with whom we minister. The few times we ventured away from his counsel we lost relationships as a result. Far better, said he, to give gifts outright than to give loans.

nancial aid. Instead we give them food items or necessary household goods.[169]

10. If we have the burden and ability to contribute to a public community project in some way, whether once (such as a mosquito net drive in areas devastated by malaria) or regularly (such as medical clinics), the funding for the project must be kept out of the national local churches. Such giving needs to be personal and separate from local church ministry.

11. We must not allow our habits of giving within the local churches to encourage financial dependency upon us or any other sources of funding outside the local assembly. In other words, our personal giving to the ministry must not be so great as to create dependence and discourage the local believers from giving themselves.[170]

The Doctrine of the Holy Spirit

I would like to raise another theological issue in regard to methodology, the doctrine of the Holy Spirit. Brothers and Sisters, when our Lord Jesus Christ gave the Church the Great Commission, did He command His disciples to go immediately about the task of making disciples in all the earth? No, He made it very clear: they were to remain in Jerusalem until they received the indwelling presence and enabling power of the Holy Spirit.[171] Only then could they proceed in obedience of the Great Commission. What are the implications of this reality?

The only thing required to fulfill the Great Commission is the verbal witness of Spirit-filled believers. The presence of the Holy Spirit in His people

---

169   Jesus told us to always give to those that ask. Jesus expects us to respond to someone who is truly destitute by giving to him what he needs for his next meal (Matt. 5:42). We cannot claim God's love and turn away from such a person without helping them. We can decide how best to give. We are not bound to give what we are asked to give or even the same amount asked for.

170   This leads to the discussion of what foreign missionaries are to do with their tithes and offerings if their giving would create a patron-client relationship in the mission work they are starting. Missionaries find themselves in a unique position because of these issues.

171   Luke 24:45–49; Acts 1:8

and the power of the Word of God is all that is needed to obey Christ and to finish the work.[172] If we conclude that something more is required to do this work, then a great majority of God's people world-wide are rendered incapable of fulfilling God's command unless they can obtain it! It would mean that the Word of God and the convincing power of the Holy Spirit are insufficient! God's ways are often much simpler than what we assume. His ways are much less dependent upon human ingenuity and strategy than we are sometimes willing to admit.

Any philosophy of outreach or missionary methodology that adds something else beyond the verbal and living witness of God's people as essential to the Great Commission is theologically aberrant. Nowhere in the New Testament apostolic record are we led to believe that anything beyond the spoken Word through Spirit-indwelled people was necessary to achieve Christ's work in saving the nations. Even the miracles and signs that are mentioned in the New Testament are portrayed as occasional and non-essential to the work of the Gospel.

Any paradigm for missions that requires enormous funding and professional expertise for something other than the proclamation of the Gospel has strayed from New Testament instruction and example.[173] Any methodology that assumes institutionalized charity as being essential to the ministry of the Gospel has also been severed from biblical moorings.

I have had a number of Cambodians, even Christians, tell me plainly that our efforts in Cambodia are destined for failure. What was their rationale? The unbelievers see that the only people they know who profess Christ are those who need some kind of material service from the Christians. They conclude that any attempt to proselytize that does not include some kind

---

172   Roland Allen gives a strong exhortation to the Church along these lines in his book *Missionary Methods: St. Paul's or Ours?* (Eerdmans Press, 1962). I would like to suggest that no missionary who is thinking through these issues should fail to read this work and consider its application to their own ministry.

173   A perhaps lesser-known work edited by R. Piece Beaver entitled *To Advance the Gospel: Rufus Anderson* (Eerdmans 1967) provides a wealth of insight into the role and priorities of a foreign missionary. Rufus Anderson was the director of a mission board for many years and is known as one of the fathers of the "indigenous principles movement" in missions.

of material or educational leverage cannot succeed. The national Christians? Most of the missionary efforts that they have seen use some kind of social aid benefit alongside proclamation, and most of the professed Christians they know have or are profiting from this exchange.[174]

What is their conclusion? To preach the Gospel without "opening hearts" first through some kind of financial benefit is unthinkable. Therefore many national leaders scramble to obtain foreign aid or assistance, or learn English, in order to "empower" their evangelism. Faith for evangelism success

---

"A missionary's methods can betray a lack of faith in the Spirit's work."

---

comes not from an unshakeable belief in the power of the Gospel and the indwelling Holy Spirit; instead faith is placed in the power of money and its ability to influence people through felt needs.

What a joy it is when Cambodian believers who came to Christ through the simple preaching of the Gospel gather together! They look around the room and realize that the power of God drew each of them to the Savior through nothing more than the simple Gospel message. They see that they were won to Christ through nothing more than the influence of the Spirit through the Word of God and the example of transformed lives. This elevates the power of the Gospel! This encourages God's people in the ability of God's Spirit to work through them to lead others to the Savior!

---

174 Some might appeal to Jesus' use of miracles in His ministry as legitimizing this approach in modern missions. Previous discussion in the book answers this in part. The ministry of Jesus had different purposes and goals than that of the Church. Jesus was proving His Messianic identity and revealing his deity through His miracles. Jesus was not "church planting" in His earthly ministry. Neither was He trying to remove societal ills or transform culture. He was revealing Himself as the Messiah and as the Son of God made flesh.

A missionary's methods can betray a lack of faith in the Spirit's work. Michael Pocock, summarizing Roland Allen's moving appeal to return to apostolic example, states:

> "This failure to trust the work of the Spirit in and among new believers was at the heart of missionaries' failure to allow indigenous leadership, teaching, financial responsibility and expansion to move forward spontaneously."[175]

My point in all of this is not to argue that a missionary should not, for instance, use medical clinics or respond to an immediate local crisis with aid. What I am referring to is the idea that such things are *necessary* in order to fulfill the Great Commission. I am also arguing that such activities are not even necessary from a strategic standpoint.

The Holy Spirit uses His people who proclaim His Word, but it is true that often trust must be built and relationships established in order for God's people to gain a hearing. When it comes to making contacts and building

---

"Where dependency and patron-client relationships have become the norm, biblical Christianity cannot flourish ..."

---

relationships, many missionaries seem to assume that some kind of organizational charity or development program must be used. I would like to suggest that this is not necessary in most places.

Why don't we take advantage of what is around us and get involved in the community, using the structures that already exist? Can we take classes at the local university? How about teaching English in a secular private school on the side? Or how about volunteering in the public school system on occasion? How about the local prison? Hospital? Is it possible that missionary

---

175   Plummer, Robert L. and Terry, John Mark. (2012). *Paul's Missionary Methods: In His Time and Ours* (Kindle Locations 1568–1569). Downers Grove, IL: IVP Academic.

children could be enrolled in the education system for a year or more? How about getting involved in a local sports club? Maybe some could consider using public transportation exclusively instead of owning a private vehicle. Is there a way to offer volunteer translation or translator services to public offices? How about the state orphanage? Maybe we could teach music lessons there or make clothing for the children. Take youth on outings, day trips to enjoy things in the area. Visit the sick and show love to the grieving around us. Start a math club in the local junior high school or at home. There are so many options at our disposal. If we build relationships in such ways, not only is it more natural and far less expensive, we avoid so many of the problems mentioned earlier in the book. God will always use such efforts, for His Holy Spirit indwells us and the fruit of His presence is clearly seen. The national believers can then see such efforts as simply developing relationships for witness within the sphere of normal life—according to one's abilities and desires—something that they can do also.[176]

We must help the national believers have confidence in the Word of God and in the indwelling power of the Holy Spirit so that they will boldly witness for Christ with expectation of a harvest. If our methodology in any way leads these brethren to doubt God's ability to work through them without funding from abroad or professional expertise, we have radically failed them in discipleship, no matter how well-intended our actions might have been.

Challenges and Blessings to Pioneer Missions

Challenges:

Where dependency and patron-client relationships have become the norm, biblical Christianity cannot flourish as it ought. Missionaries who see this and try to correct it will likely find a very difficult task ahead, facing resistance by nationals used to the system and foreigners who have created and perpetuate the problem. The importance of avoiding negative precedents

---

176 Using this model, teams of missionaries can rapidly develop relationships and have contacts for the Gospel. Team members could then pursue building relationships within the community, using those avenues that are according to their individual abilities and desires.

is not often understood well by newer missionaries, and mistakes with the use of funds can be difficult to correct. More than any other matter, money issues create more strife and bad blood, both inside the Church as well as outside of it, which is why the Apostle Paul remarked, "For the love of money is a root of all kinds of evils."[177]

Blessings:

When we maintain the important dynamic of spiritual relationships with the national believers, we experience equal fellowship with them in Christ and enjoy freedom in ministry. It is a true joy to see national churches that are truly indigenous, free from financial dependence and patronage from abroad, functioning as God intended in the New Testament. When national leaders that you have taught can disagree with you, correct you, rebuke you, or even ignore you because you have no control over them outside of the Scriptures—rejoice!

---

177   1 Tim. 6:10

Factor 8:
Changing times can obscure unchanging needs.

Out with the Old and In with the New?

Today's "Super Missionary" travels to one of today's unreached peoples, armed with the knowledge that there are virtually no Christians. He is zealous to get to work preaching the Gospel, glorying that he has the opportunity to preach Christ where He is not named. Once he settles in, however, he finds that other believers have already sown some Gospel seed through various creative ways. Maybe some from that area have gone abroad to work or study and have begun to witness to family back home. Maybe Christian radio has been broadcasting or Christian movies have been shown on television. It might even be that Christian tourists or short-termers have passed out large amounts of Gospel tracts in the area. All of this might have taken place with no Christian workers on the ground and precious few churches established. The Super Missionary becomes deflated because he thought he was going to virgin territory!

Pioneer missions are being greatly impacted by globalization.[178] None of us have failed to notice that mission work is no longer like it was in the days of Adoniram Judson where the only light or witness was the foreign missionary who was physically present. In those days most peoples of the earth did not travel far, and few were literate. Missionaries or Christian witnesses from other countries crossing cultures for ministry or business were precious few indeed. Times have indeed changed.

Globalization's impact has changed missions in many places. People are having the Gospel sown and watered among them in numerous ways unknown to our fathers in past generations. There are many things happening

---

178   By globalization, we refer to how the world is getting smaller and more integrated through technology and business.

today that create much more opportunity for Gospel proclamation than ever before:

- people in limited-access countries emigrating to lands with religious freedom
- students going abroad to pursue higher education in "Christian" countries
- Christians adopting children from restricted-access nations or unreached peoples
- refugees finding the Gospel in the camps and wherever they flee to in the West
- the internet exploding with evangelistic opportunity for anyone remotely seeking Christ
- computers providing opportunity for Christian resources to be copied, seen, and heard by far more people than the printed page, and translation services far easier to come by
- English as the global business language opening up communication in ways not known throughout world history
- international churches meeting in many of the large cities of the world, reaching people from many nations
- teachers and preachers of the Word of God easily traveling around the world in very little time
- Christians establishing businesses in closed countries and living there permanently as witnesses, etc.

We have not even begun to discuss short-term missions! Globalization is causing evangelism to be a group effort in the Church like never before. We need to praise God for this!

In our own limited ministry in Cambodia, the mingling of nations has added to our opportunities even in our out-of-the-way location. Here are some examples of such opportunities: a number of doctors have come to do research projects on malaria in our province's state hospital, including a Chinese man who actually had a Christian relative back in China; a weak believer from South Korea who was on contract in our town of Pursat doing aid work; an Englishman and I had breakfast together where we discussed the Gospel; opportunities to witness to Norwegians, Canadians, Nigerian and Cameroonian Africans, and even a number of Israeli Jews!

We have been blessed to have a part in spreading the Gospel via the internet through sermons we have preached and uploaded—over twenty-three thousand downloads as of this writing, primarily from Cambodians all over the world. These bear witness to the potential of what is possible as people hungry for the Word find His truth online.[179]

Avoid Getting Sidetracked from a Primary Need

We must rejoice in the positive aspects of globalization's impact on missions, taking advantage of the opportunities of our times. We must remind ourselves that these modern blessings do provide exciting avenues for Gospel witness, but they do not replace the critical need for long-term cross-cultural Christian missions. Pioneer missionaries who know the language and culture of the people are integral for doing the work we as a Church are commanded to do. God is still in the business of raising up evangelists and church planters and spiritually gifting them for that primary task of laying the foundation of the Gospel. Their job is to zealously labor to make disciples and then organize them into local bodies of believers who will then represent Christ by believing and living the Gospel together.

Evangelism as it is commonly understood does not fulfill the Great Commission. Getting the information of the Gospel to people in unreached places is not the task given to us by our Lord. Making disciples is.[180] This requires men and women committed to leading the lost to repentance and faith and teaching them how to live for their new God and Savior. Laying a Gospel foundation is not possible without making disciples. For this reason, there is still a great need to send full-time cross-cultural missionaries to many places in the world, both for church planting and the training of lead-

---

179 Consider how you might be able to use sites like *www.sermonaudio.com*, *www.facebook.com, or www.youtube.com* for evangelism on a foreign field.

180 Praise the Lord for the many pastors who are being revived in their understanding and practice of discipleship today. We need to make sure that we apply this to foreign missions as well!

ers.[181] In other places, the foundation of the Gospel has already been laid, so the national church may only need strengthening or equipping ministries.

Short-term laborers can certainly assist in evangelism and even discipleship to some degree, but the level of discipleship required for laying the foundation of the Gospel effectively is going to come from pioneer laborers who fulfill their long-term calling with understanding. They live and minister in the heart language and understand the religion and culture of the people with whom they are ministering.

Ultimately, the Word of God is always effective, always working out the purposes of God. We must praise God for every way in which His Word is being spread around the world. None of these efforts are wasted![182]

Having said this, we must be honest with ourselves and accept that there are real limitations on the effectiveness of those seeking to make disciples and train leaders using short-term methods. Teaching students who are listening in their second or third language, even if it is English, is not ideal. Teaching through translators is not natural communication and has limited value. Even translating materials written for other times and cultures are not nearly as effective as those materials written and published in the language of the people, materials which reflect that culture's needs. Why? Those materials are addressing needs and answering questions for a specific cultural context and thus have limited value. Different cultural contexts require different resources—the same truths, just packaged differently to meet the need.

Christian videos, Christian music, internet sermons, special evangelistic meetings, Gospel tracts, etc., all help in the sowing of the Gospel, but these are no replacement for preachers of the Gospel, living Christian witnesses, who can teach and live out Christianity before the lost where they live. We use *www.sermonaudio.com* and have rejoiced at limited results from such a

---

181   An American missionary in Thailand, Karl Dahlfred, argues for this ongoing need on his blog (*http://dahlfred.com/en/blogs/gleanings-from-the-field/131-are-long-term-missionaries-obsolete*). This is an excellent source for thinking through Southeast Asian Buddhist missions issues.

182   Isa. 55:10–11

simple means. We have used MegaVoice solar-powered audio Bibles[183] as a way to get the Word of God into the hands of those who would not allow us to witness directly or who had already received seed. All such things are helps, but living witnesses cannot be replaced.

Most short-termers come to the mission field wanting to serve or contribute in some meaningful way. By this they mean preaching, counseling, building something, or volunteering in some humanitarian way. In our ministry, we have found that the most effective ministry that foreign visitors can have is to engage in reciprocal ministry. What I mean is, everything that the visitors do, the local believers do as well. If a foreigner preaches to the church through a translator, then a local pastor or believer also preaches to the congregation and visitors. If the foreigners sing special songs, so do the locals. If the visitors give testimonies, so do the nationals. If the short-termers pray, the local believers also pray. This is *reciprocal* ministry, true *spiritual* fellowship. There is no patronage, no inequality. This lifts up the national church and expresses their dignity with us and oneness in Christ much more than financial gifts. We have seen this emphasis prove a great blessing, both to visitors and locals alike.

Those short-termers that visit with a longing in their hearts to learn about missions and understand what missionaries actually do will not fail to find their trip profitable. This will impact their discernment in giving to missions, focus their prayer ministry for missionaries and peoples, and clarify in their minds whether or not God is leading them to be one of those that go cross-culturally for the Gospel. Many, however, do not go to learn. Their entire focus is upon what they can "do" to make an impact. I will argue that the greatest impact that most short-termers can have lies in these two areas mentioned: spiritual fellowship with the national believers, and increased understanding about missions ministry.

---

183   *http://www.megavoice.com/*. We have found that units such as these are especially helpful in introducing illiterate people to the Gospel, as well as in their initial discipleship when they first believe.

Remember That Sacrifice Is Central to the Task of Pioneer Missions

Short-term teaching and training and other efforts abroad have been used of the Lord and will continue to be. Globalization increases such opportunities and makes them even easier. Even so, many men and women must commit to learning languages and cultures in order to have the greatest level of effectiveness. They must be willing to sacrifice and die to self in the pursuit of making the greatest difference they possibly can. Pioneer fields need this kind of Gospel laborer above all else. Laying solid foundations of the Gospel among the unreached requires it. We must continue to send out, support, and pray for these kinds of laborers!

Why is this so important? When we learn a people's language, we also learn their culture, for these two are intimately related. Through language we begin to understand the worldview of the people—how they think about religion, how they use religious terms, how they view the supernatural, family, time, politics, entertainment, work, life, death, relationships, education, money, marriage, music, food, worship, honor, vice, the arts, etc. I have heard people involved in missions say, "People are just people. Sin is the same and people are the same, no matter where you are. We do not really need to know language or culture to teach the Bible effectively." While there is some truth in these statements, do we really believe this?

While on a recent furlough I tried to witness to an Albanian Muslim taxi driver in Chicago and found it was not easy to engage him with the Gospel. When was the last time you tried to engage a Chinese ancestor worshipper? Have you tried to have a Bible study with a Hindu? Honesty requires that we take this matter seriously, understanding its implications on short-term missions.

Again, I do not mean by this that there is no place for short-term missions or teaching of God's Word through a translator. I do mean, however, to call attention to *the priority* of full-time cross-cultural laborers. Maybe some of those engaged in short-term work should consider pursuing full-time work instead. It could be that some should learn languages and cultures among peoples they are trying to reach, even if their missions are short term. Short-term missionaries should collaborate with long-term missionaries to determine how best to use their time, energy, and gifts effectively. We need to work together in this foundational task of making disciples among unreached peoples.

Suggestions for the use of English in non-English speaking countries[184]

As we reflect on the use of English on the mission field, and consider all of the ways that we have seen and heard of English being used here in Cambodia and elsewhere, we suggest the following guidelines:

- Our goal should be to minister to people spiritually in their first language wherever possible. We must do everything that we can to encourage and support cross-cultural laborers who know the heart language and culture of the people whom they are trying to reach and disciple.[185]
- Rely on national believers and long-term missionaries who know the language for most spiritual ministry. Limit the use of translators wherever possible.[186]

---

184   English is not the only foreign language being used in missions today. In Cambodia, English and Korean are both being used by many Christian workers.

185   We realize that this is not always possible because of difficult political situations. Large international communities also need to be reached in the cities, and many of these speak English or another host country language as their second language. Placing laborers in such ministries to cover every ethnic group and language is not possible. However, many steps can be made to help bridge the cultural and linguistic gap. An international ministry in Bangkok, for instance, should have pastors that speak Thai since that is the host culture's language, and many of the internationals will speak Thai and intermarry with Thais. A multi-ethnic ministry in a predominantly Asian area of Los Angeles could be sure to include pastors that are Asian or who speak one of the Asian languages spoken in that community. Such decisions would greatly increase the potential effectiveness of discipleship efforts.

186   God has, does, and will use His people who preach and teach His Word through less effective means—praise be to His name that He does! However, what we are discussing

- Use short-term English teachers as a means to gain contacts for those missionaries living and ministering in a place permanently. The Spirit-filled lives and limited witness of the mature Christian short-termers can be used to build relationships and encourage people to begin to consider Christ.
- Short-term English teachers should charge for their services so that they can subsidize their time on the field, rather than take up resources that could be used to support full-time missionaries.
- Those missionaries who teach English should restrict this secular activity to public places or private homes, not where the church meets for worship. This avoids confusion regarding the purpose of the local church and why people attend there for worship.
- English teaching should be "no strings attached." English should never be used as leverage to get non-Christians to go to church or Christian activities. For example, a number of ministries in Cambodia offer free English teaching, but only to those who faithfully attend church on Sunday. That approach cheapens the Gospel in the eyes of the unbelievers and reveals a lack of faith in the power of the Holy Spirit.

The 1 Corinthians 9 Principle

Cross-cultural missionaries who are willing to labor for the Lord Jesus Christ on pioneer mission fields must embrace the 1 Corinthians 9:19–27 principle: "I must be all things to all men with all discipline of body and spirit that I might win some."[187]

In Cambodia we have seen many who are willing to come teach English, build buildings, work in cafes, dig wells, give time and resources to devel-

---

here is what is most effective, what God's people should be striving for and supporting with the greatest zeal.

187   If you are considering foreign missions, 1 Corinthians is a manual on how to apply the Gospel in a pagan culture. 1 & 2 Corinthians provide a manual on the role of the missionary preacher of the Gospel. Few things can be more helpful to the missionary or prospective missionary than a thorough study of this principle in the context of 1 Corinthians 9 and how it can relate to foreign missionaries today.

opment organizations, or do medical missions trips for a week or two; but men and women are needed who are committed to the labors of the Gospel and possess the spirit we find in the Apostle Paul in 1 Corinthians 9. Men and women set apart for the Gospel (those separated out by God for proclamation, discipleship, and training of national believers) must lay down their personal rights and embrace a life of discipline for Jesus' sake.

The most basic and first-level fulfillment of the Great Commission is church planting on pioneer fields. Many must wholly give themselves to this work with all discipline of body and spirit by the grace of God. God's people must lay aside their "rights" for the sake of Christ's name and be willing to do the hardest things for Him!

When Paul gives his illustrations in 1 Corinthians 9 about the Isthmian games runner and boxer, he does so in the context of explaining his view of himself as a pioneer missionary apostle. Pioneer missions requires a lifestyle of labor, toil, discipline, self-denial, intense motivation, and focus. The primary application of the closing verses of this chapter is for those engaged in pioneer missions![188]

"I must be all things to all men with all discipline of body and spirit that I might win some."

What was Paul really saying in this missionary passage when he said that he tried to be all things to all men? To what lengths was he willing to go? He was not describing his willingness to sacrifice the message, but his willingness to sacrifice himself to preach the message. He would give up everything—even become "a slave to all"—if that would promote the spread of the unadulterated Gospel. His desire to win souls was the heart of this text, and he repeated it several times—"that I might win the more," "that I might

---

188   A closer look at this passage and its application to daily missionary life can be found by reading Mabel Williamson of China Inland Mission's book *Have We No Rights?* (Moody Press, 1957). I urge all who are involved in foreign missions to read this little book, which is available on Kindle.

win Jews," "that I might win those who are under the law," "that I might win those who are without law," "that I might win the weak," and "that I may by all means save some." So winning people to Christ was his one objective. In order to do that, Paul was willing to give up all his rights and privileges, his position, his rank, his livelihood, his freedom—ultimately even his life. If it would further the spread of the Gospel, Paul would claim no rights, make no demands, and insist on no privileges.[189]

And that is precisely how Paul lived and ministered. He did not modify the message to suit the world, but he made sure that he personally was never an obstacle to anyone's hearing and understanding the message of Christ. He was describing an attitude of personal sacrifice, not compromise. He never altered the clear and confronting call to repentance and faith.[190]

Wherever he could acknowledge the traditions of a people and not offend their sensitivities, Paul was glad to do so—when it did not violate God's

---

"Whatever the circumstances, God's priorities must be maintained, and the ministry of the Gospel must not be allowed to be redefined."

Word or impinge on the Gospel. But the apostle never adapted his ministry to pander to worldly lusts or sinful selfishness.[191] He wanted to remove any personal offense, so the offense of the Gospel would be the only one.[192]

---

189 This does not mean that Paul did not ever exercise his rights or abide by personal preferences or desires. This discussion has to do with those rights, preferences, or desires (aspects of our personality) that potentially hinder ministry in a given situation. Where our rights, preferences or desires do not create obstacles to faith in the lives of others, we can live accordingly, as long as those things honor Christ (1 Cor. 10:31).

190 MacArthur, Jr., J. F. (1993). *Ashamed of the Gospel: When the Church Becomes Like the World,* p. 92. Wheaton, IL: Crossway Books.

191 Ibid., p. 99.

192 Ibid., p. 100.

There are many missionaries today that are either unwilling or unable to follow this 1 Corinthians 9 principle because lifestyle issues are far too important to them. This failure means they cannot operate according to what is communicated in this book—even if they agreed with it philosophically.

It is crucial for foreign missionaries to maintain a lifestyle that is not materialistic. Our lifestyle must not be perceived as materialistic *by the nationals,* not just ourselves. Those whose daily lifestyle is considered extravagant from the perspective of the nationals will bring upon themselves criticism, resentment, and the weight of unnecessary guilt. Their very motives for pursuing their ministry will be challenged. The 1 Corinthians 9 principle requires that missionaries take this matter seriously. How missionaries should apply this principle will vary from culture to culture and even differ within a culture based upon where one lives.

Mabel Williamson's book is full of helpful explanation and applications regarding the 1 Corinthians 9 principle. She says this:

> "On the mission field it is not the enduring of hardships, the lack of comforts, and the roughness of the life that make the missionary cringe and falter. It is something far less romantic and far more real. It is something that will hit you right down where you live. The missionary has to give up having his own way."[193]

No matter how world circumstances change, 1 Corinthians 9 missionaries will be needed throughout the world until the fullness of the Gentiles comes in.[194] Times are indeed changing; with this globalization also comes greater control of governments over their people. It is becoming increasingly difficult to pursue pioneer missions under a simple religious worker status. Creativity will increasingly be required in the pursuit of missions. Secular employment or social action may provide the needed door to obtain visas or residency. Whatever the circumstances, God's priorities must be maintained, and the ministry of the Gospel must not be allowed to be redefined. An application of this principle of being all things to all men is maintaining

---

193   Williamson, Mabel. *Have We No Rights? A frank discussion of the "rights" of missionaries.* Kindle Edition.

194   Rom. 11:25

a reproducible methodology of church planting, regardless of the cultural circumstances the missionary finds himself in.

Others will need to be bi-vocational for financial or strategic reasons. What is referred to as tent-making missions will no doubt become more the norm if biblical Christianity continues to shrink in the more affluent sending countries. Regardless of a church planter's work status, whether fully employed in secular work, bi-vocational, or fully supported by God's people, what I communicate in this book is relevant and reproducible. If it is biblical, then this must be so.

Challenges and Blessings to Pioneer Missions

Challenges:

Pioneer missionaries need wisdom about how to effectively use modern technology to encourage the work of the Gospel. They need discernment about how to encourage and discourage those that desire to pursue short-term missions on their field of labor. Maintaining commitment to the long-term work is getting harder in the context of globalization. Staying focused on a lifestyle of self-denial and fervent labor in the Gospel is difficult to maintain for both spiritual and physical reasons. Many coming from individualistic and more materialistic societies are not ready for just how often the matter of laying down one's rights must be applied.

Blessings:

It gives us joy to see how God is using His people to assist one another in ways unforeseen just a few years ago. Because of technology and globalization, potential opportunities for being a part in the fulfillment of the Great Commission have never been as numerous. As we learn to deny ourselves for the Gospel's sake, our walk with the Lord deepens as we identify with Him in His servanthood.

Conclusion: Greater Freedom, Greater Effectiveness

The task of pioneer missions faces real challenges. Most are similar to the challenges in ministry faced by many of you at home in the ministries you are a part of. As you can see, there are some distinct differences, but many of them are different only in degree. The same is true for the blessings

One thing I hope this book communicates to the mind and heart of all of its readers is this: the spiritual qualifications are *higher*, not *lower*, for those working on the mission field! Consider the words of Rufus Anderson, a missionary statesman through most of the nineteenth century, who said this concerning the pioneer missionary:

> "I even think that the mental pressure upon the intelligent and conscientious missionary is often greater than it is upon his brethren at home. For he finds that there is everything to be done, and that he is the only one to do it. He must be feet to the lame, eyes to the blind, ears to the deaf, and must almost reconstruct the intellect, and almost recreate the conscience. Did this responsibility come upon the missionary all at once, he could not bear it; but come it will, sooner or later, and the intelligent and faithful missionary need fear no loss of stimulus to his mind.... For the reason just now stated, *more strength of piety* **is required to be a good missionary among the heathen, than to be a good pastor at home.** I do not claim for the missionary a more perfect exhibition of the Christian life, than is seen in the home ministry; but since, in their exposed circumstances, **they need a higher and firmer tone of the inward Christian life ... .**" (emphasis mine).[195]

---

195   Anderson, Rufus and Beaver, R. Pierce. (1967). *To Advance the Gospel: Selected Writings in the Theory and Practice of Missions*, p. 205. Grand Rapids, MI: Wm. B. Eerdmans. I highly recommend this book as a great gift for missionaries, missions teachers, and mission directors.

I believe that missionaries who embrace the philosophy of pioneer missions in this book will experience a sense of *liberation*. Why liberation? They will understand that all that is required of Gospel laborers is to preach Christ and live out their faith wherever it is that they live and labor. Nothing else is required! Nothing else is even desirable. The weight of the world's problems because of its sin and rebellion against God is not their responsibility. They do not have to raise money for large ministry expenses. They are not required to study development strategies and oversee aid organizations in order to obey the Great Commission. They do not have to continually appeal to God's people back home for more money to fund their programs. They do not have the burden of solving all the problems in the churches or their ministries. They don't have to be strapped down by the weight of being a financial patron. Instead, they will have the freedom to function as a spiritual leader among equals, even among believers of different nationalities, backgrounds, and social standings.

I believe that pastors who embrace the philosophy of missions woven throughout this work will obtain greater *discernment*. They will look at potential missionary candidates much differently. Leaders will be more careful about who they send out in the name of Jesus to fulfill the Great Commission. They will understand that the real work of missions is spiritual and that only those spiritually qualified should be sent and supported to do such work. Godly Christian character, a mature understanding of the Christian faith, an ability to search the Scriptures for answers, humility to zealously learn a foreign language and culture, an understanding of missions issues, and a willingness to lay aside one's rights will be the primary qualifications of those they send. They will not tolerate missionaries who do not exhibit these necessary qualities. They will know how to better prepare those interested in missions.

Churches will gain a greater clarity about priorities for use of their missions funds. Those considering short-term missions trips will have greater insight into how they might be effectively used. Leaders will have greater wisdom in responding to the continual appeals for funds being made from all corners of the globe. They will realize that many of these appeals are for causes of very low priority in the big picture of what God is doing in this world. Some churches will realize that maintaining God's priorities will actually free up resources to support Gospel laborers. Others will have discovered that monies that they thought were being used for poverty relief were not really addressing genuine poverty at all. The result in some churches may be a restructuring of their giving to missions. Missionaries would have less to raise because they are not expected to support and fund works on the field Better stewardship would most likely result in church planting missionaries getting to the field much more quickly.

In many ways this book is a call to God's people to return to New Testament simplicity in fulfilling the Great Commission. It is a call to a deeply spiritual mission with its methods being those that rely upon the Holy Spirit instead

---

> ## *"Many good brethren have methods of missions that are a denial of the theology that they profess."*

---

of those that rely on the power of money to manipulate. It is a call to simplify and de-professionalize missionary methods. It is a call to rally around God's priorities by faith, no matter what pressure the world and confused Christianity brings to bear. It is a call to remember how the Scriptures define and exemplify the fulfillment of the Great Commission.

It is also a challenge to God's people to consider how our theology has everything to do with our methodology. These two should be inseparably linked. Many good brethren have methods of missions that are a denial of the theology that they profess. As missionary Karl Dahlfred writes:

> "This understanding of the intimate relationship between theology and methodology, however, has been largely lost in the contemporary Church."[196]

---

196 Dahlfred, Karl. (2012). *Theology Drives Methodology: Conversion in the Theology of Charles Finney and John Nevin* (Kindle Location 418)..

As Christopher Little writes, "As the church goes, so goes its mission."[197] We do what we do in our attempt to fulfill the Great Commission because of our current theological understanding of that mission. Many need to shore up their theology of missions, conform it to the Scriptures, and then learn how to apply that theology consistently throughout their ministries. Others have a sound theological position doctrinally; yet they have not taken the time to think through how that doctrine applies in practice in missions.[198]

If our missions practice is in a state of chaos and inconsistency, it is because our theology about missions lacks clarity and focus. If we "just take things as they come" or "shoot from the hip" in our practice of missions, it is because we still lack clear biblical principles to guide our theology of missions.

My hope is that some will see through this discussion their disconnect between their theological positions and their practice of missions, resulting in churches conforming more to the model of missions given to us in the New Testament.

> "Remember that Biblical correctness is the *only* framework by which we must evaluate all ministry methods. Any end-justifies-the-means philosophy inevitably *will* compromise doctrine, despite any proviso to the contrary. If we make effectiveness the gauge of right and wrong, how can that fail to color our doctrine? Ultimately the pragmatist's notion of truth is shaped by what seems effective, not by the objective revelation of Scripture."[199]

---

197   Little, Christopher. (2005). *Mission in the Way of Paul: Biblical Mission for the Church in the Twenty-first Century*, p. 234. Peter Lang.

198   The philosophy of missions that is expressed in this book is in complete harmony with my biblical convictions as a Baptist. When a Baptist missionary or churches operate their missions ministry according to other paradigms, it reveals to this author a weak understanding or belief in those doctrines that Baptists are supposed to hold dear. Among other things, Baptist ecclesiology emphasizes New Testament simplicity and local church autonomy.

199   MacArthur, Jr., J. F. (1993). *Ashamed of the Gospel: When the Church Becomes Like the World*, p. 78. Wheaton, IL: Crossway Books.

"It is folly to think one can be both pragmatic *and* biblical. The pragmatist wants to know *what works now*. The biblical thinker cares only about *what the Bible mandates*. The two philosophies oppose each other at the most basic level."[200]

Brethren, we are safe when we anchor our methodology in the commands and examples given to us by the New Testament Church. The more we add to this simplicity through our penchant for ingenuity and institutionalism, the farther we get away from God's ways and blessings. The ministry of the Gospel as exemplified to us in the New Testament is simple, yet profound. Let us embrace this simplicity by faith and let the Holy Spirit do the profound work through the grace of Jesus Christ. Let us lay aside those weights which hinder our effectiveness as we seek to do battle in places of darkness. The spiritual battle on pioneer mission fields is intense enough in its own right; let us not increase the difficulty by making the task more complicated than God meant for it to be. Let us do our part and rest in His grace and mercy as He works out His eternal plan of salvation throughout the earth for His glory!

If we will meet the challenges of pioneer missions in the grace of Christ, we, and others through us, will have the joy of sharing in its blessings.[201]

---

200 Ibid., p. 79–80.

201 1 Cor. 9:23

Appendix:
Run or Fight?

What about those missionaries who feel trapped in a ministry situation that was not founded on this New Testament understanding of missions? What about places where the church has been raised upon a weak foundation because former missionaries failed to understand their task? Are we to abandon such churches since they are now so problematic, so set in their ways? Should we give ourselves and expend time and energy correcting ministries that are reaping ill consequences because of unfortunate methodologies sown in times past?

If the Gospel foundation has not been laid in truth by previous missionaries, we must not abandon the field. We must be willing to do the hard work of striving to lay that foundation of Gospel truth, even in the face of dealing with the added layers of trouble caused in the past. This task is non-negotiable.

But what about those fields where Gospel truth was preached clearly and faithfully, but missionary methodology promoted rampant dependency and encouraged patron-client relationships which left behind an anemic church? M. David Sills writes these words to address this situation:

> "Missionaries who study missiology[202] and modern methods in a world that has the advantage of reflection on preceding generations' research and experience often arrive in mission field settings where … ministries they inherit are not what the missionaries wish they were. Perhaps the first missionaries ministered during the days of 'missionary compound mentality,' or of replicating the sending church from another country, or using financial resources to maintain control and loyalty among the national church. None of the earlier missionaries intended negative results or patronizing men-

---

202 Missiology is simply the study or science of missions. It includes all of what the Scriptures teach about missions, the history of missions, missionary strategy, and the study of language and culture.

talities, but they occurred and remained just the same. Some newer missionaries often feel it would be easier to go and start afresh elsewhere. What should the new missionary in such a setting do? Allen wrote of this challenge for the young missionary with a different perspective,

'He cannot possibly ignore that situation. He cannot act as if the Christian community over which he is called to preside had had another history. He cannot desert them and run away to some untouched field. He cannot begin all over again. Nevertheless, if he has the Spirit of St. Paul he can in a very real sense practice the method of St. Paul in its nature, if not in its form. He cannot undo the past, but he can amend the present. He can keep ever before his mind the truth that he is there to prepare the way for the retirement of the foreign missionary. He can live his life amongst his people and deal with them as though he would have no successor. He should remember that he is the least permanent element in the church. He may fall sick and go home, or he may die, or he may be called elsewhere. He disappears, the church remains.'"[203]

"It is possible for a missionary to enter a ministry setting where contextualization was not done, where dysfunctional relationships or beliefs are rampant, and to first de-contextualize and then properly re-contextualize. This will not be easy, but it can be done. Only when the Gospel, Christianity, and Christian ministry are understood and practiced in culturally appropriate and sensible ways will the missionaries be able to say that they have finished the task. The Great Commission is to reach and teach others everything Christ commanded, discipling them. Only with this goal of critical contextualization are missionaries truly able to take the things God has taught them and 'entrust to faithful men who will be able to teach others also' (2 Tim. 2:2)."[204]

---

203 Plummer, Robert L., and Terry, John Mark. (2012). *Paul's Missionary Methods: In His Time and Ours* (Kindle Locations 2248–2253). Downers Grove, IL: IVP Academic.

204 Ibid., Kindle Locations 2254–2258.

If the Apostle Paul were alive today, Christopher Little argues, he "would labor resolutely to dismantle the dependency syndrome which presently characterizes the relationship between the Western and non-Western churches. Paul never had to confront the dependency syndrome because he wisely avoided creating it."[205] With wise perception, Little further states:

> "his idea of expressing church unity entailed the sharing of spiritual gifts among the people of God (Ac. 13:1; Rom. 1:11; 12:4–8; 1 Co. 12:4–7; Eph. 4:11–13) rather than any continuous flow of material resources from one church to another …. For whatever the reasons, the church in mission has generally departed from Paul's philosophy of ministry in this area. As a consequence, it has given birth to the modern phenomena called the syndrome of dependency."[206]

I agree with Little's assessment. Obviously, in regards to the syndrome of dependency plaguing missions, our situation today is much different than that of the Apostle Paul. Little adds,

> "Because more monetary wealth is being passed from one section of the church to another than any time in history, one is left to conclude that the church is most likely experiencing the most paternalistic age it has ever known."[207]

Our response must not be defeatism but passion to make a difference wherever God places us in the fulfillment of His Great Commission.

Help is available for brethren seeking to fulfill this challenging task.[208] But more important than practical help is faith in the power of God and His

---

205   Little, Christopher. (2005). *Mission in the Way of Paul: Biblical Mission for the Church in the Twenty-first Century*, p. 238. Peter Lang.

206   Ibid., p. 238.

207   Ibid., p. 240.

208   A mission agency whose primary purpose is to help missionaries and national churches extract themselves from the unfortunate consequences of financial patron-client relationships is World Missions Associates in Lancaster, PA, founded by Glenn Schwartz. Their website, *http://www.wmausa.org/*, has many helpful materials. Glenn's book *When Charity Destroys Dignity: Overcoming Unhealthy Dependency in the Christian Movement*

Word to renew His people, and the patience and self-denial needed to see the work accomplished by the grace of God. With God all things are possible.[209]

Remember the landmine analogy of Jean Johnson given in the introduction? The analogy addressed "missiological landmines," many of which we have sought to call attention to in this book. We have not yet, however, talked about the de-miners. I have seen plenty of de-mining operations, camps, vehicles, and employees during our time here. These de-mining teams are still at work, especially in the part of the country that I live in now.

What do the de-miners do? Well-trained, courageous, and very careful de-miners use detecting equipment to find unexploded ordnances. When they find them, they mark them well for all to see, often using a red sign with the symbol of skull and crossbones. They often rope off the area as well and then begin the slow and meticulous process of detonation and removal of the ordnances. It is grueling work and injuries, even death, sometimes result.

Missionaries working on mission fields that have been sown with missiological landmines can be compared to these de-miners. The missiological landmines simply must be removed, by the grace of God, in order for the foundation of the Gospel to be effectively laid. Knowledge, courage, discernment, and above all, faith, are required to tackle the slow and difficult process of de-mining. Missionaries and national pastors need to courageously strive together to get rid of these mines, or casualties will continue to mount in the Church, the gospel foundational will continue to be weakened, and God's glory continue to be diminished.

If, in God's sovereign plan, He chooses not to give us visible success in that for which we labor, we will not lose the reward given to those preachers of the Gospel that labored faithfully,[210] who "did not shrink back from declar-

---

(AuthorHouse, 2007) deals with dependency and the urgent need for self-reliance in national churches.

209   Matt. 19:26; Lk. 1:37

210   1 Cor. 4:1–2

ing the whole counsel of God."[211] There will be less human glory for such a ministry, but this is not the praise that we seek.[212] It may be that God is calling some reading this to pursue this kind of difficult ministry for Jesus' sake.

---

211 Acts 20:27

212 1 Cor. 4:1–5; 2 Cor.4:1–2

Bibliography

Books and articles concerning missions:

The Holy Spirit. (Eternal). *The Holy Scriptures.*

Agar, Michael. (2002). *Language Shock: Understanding the Culture of Conversation.* Perennial.

Allen, Rolland. (2002). *Missionary Methods: St. Paul's or Ours?* Grand Rapids: Wm. B. Eerdmans. (Original work published 1962).

Beaver, R. Pierce, Ed. (1967). *To Advance the Gospel: Selections From the Writings of Rufus Anderson.* Grand Rapids: Wm. B. Eerdmans.

Doran, Dave. (2002). *For the Sake of His Name: Challenging a new generation for world missions.* Allen Park, MI: Student Global Impact.

Glenny, W. Edward and William H. Smallman, Eds. (2000). *Missions in a New Millennium: Change & Challenges in World Missions.* Grand Rapids: Kregel.

Hiebert, Paul G., Shaw, R. Daniel, Tienou, Tite. (1999). *Understanding Folk Religion: A Christian Response to Popular Beliefs and Practices.* Baker Books.

Hesselgrave, David. (2000, 2nd ed.). *Planting Churches Cross-Culturally: North America & Beyond.* Grand Rapids: Baker Academic.

Hesselgrave, David. (2006). *Paradigms in Conflict: 10 Key Questions in Christian Missions Today. Grand Rapids.* MI: Kregel Academic.

Hodges, Melvin. (1999). *The Indigenous Church: A Complete Handbook On How to Grow Young Churches.* Springfield, MO: Gospel Publishing House. (Original work written in 1953).

Johnson, Jean. (2012). *We Are Not the Heroes: A Missionary's Guide for Sharing Christ, Not a Culture of Dependency.* Deep River Books.

Johnson, Jesse (Sept. 27, 2011). "Mercy Ministry is Not Kingdom Work" *Cripplegate* blog: *http://thecripplegate.com/.*

Little, Christopher R. (2005). *Mission in the Way of Paul: Biblical Missions for the Church in the Twenty-First Century.* New York: Peter Lang Publishing.

McIlwain, Trevor. (2001). *Building on Firm Foundations: Guidelines for Evangelism and Teaching Believers.* Sanford, FL: New Tribes Mission. (Original work published 1987).

McPhail, Forrest, Seawright, Chris. "Stewardship in Foreign Missions: Should Foreigners Support National Leaders?" *The Visitor,* June-July

2007. (See also: *http://obfvisitor.wordpress.com/2007/06/01/stewardship-in-foreign-missions-part-1/#more-61*).

Nevius, John. (2003). *The Planting and Development of Missionary Churches.* Hancock, NH: Monadnock Press. (Original work pubished in Shanghai, China, 1886).

Nevius, John and Helen. (2010). *The Life of John Livingston Nevius: For Forty Years a Missionary in China.* Nabu Press. (Original work published in 1923).

Payne, J. D. (2009). *Discovering Church Planting: An Introduction to the Whats, Whys, and Hows of Global Church Planting.* Paternoster.

Piper, John. (2004, 2nd ed). *Let the Nations Be Glad! The Supremacy of God in Missions.* Grand Rapids: Baker Academic.

Plummer, Robert L. and Terry, John Mark. (2012). *Paul's Missionary Methods: In His Time and Ours.* IVP Academic.

Schnabel, Eckhard. (2008). *Paul the Missionary: Realities, Strategies, and Methods.* IVP Academic.

Schwartz, Glenn. (2007). *When Charity Destroys Dignity: Overcoming Unhealthy Dependency in the Christian Movement.* Bloomington, IN: Author House.

Taylor, Geraldine. (1998). *Behind the Ranges: The Life-Changing Story of J.O. Fraser.* Singapore: OMF International. (Original work published 1944).

Warren, Max, Ed. (1971). *To Apply the Gospel: Selections From the Writings of Henry Venn.* Grand Rapids: Wm. B. Eerdmans.

Williamson, Mabel. (1957). *Have We No Rights?* Moody Press.

Books and articles addressing wider theological issues that affect missions:

Barry, J. D., M. R. Grigoni, M. S Heiser, M. Custis, D. Mangum, and M. M. Whitehead. (2012). *Faithlife Study Bible.* Bellingham, WA: Logos Bible Software.

Chance, B. (2003). "Fellowship," *Holman Illustrated Bible Dictionary.* Nashville, TN: Holman Bible Publishers.

Diprose, Ronald E. (2000). *Israel and the Church: The Origins and Effects of Replacement Theology.* Authentic Media.

MacArthur, Jr. J.F. (1993). *Ashamed of the Gospel: When the Church Becomes Like the World.* Wheaton, IL: Crossway Books.

MacArthur, Jr. J.F. (1995). *Rediscovering Pastoral Ministry*. Word Publishing.

Murray, Ian. (1998). *Pentecost Today? The Biblical Basis for Understanding Revival*. Banner of Truth Trust.

McCune, Rolland. (2004). *Promise Unfulfilled: The Failed Strategy of Modern Evangelicalism*. Ambassador Emerald International.

Johnson, Jesse. "Discontinuity: the poor, Israel, and the Church", Sept. 20, 2011. Blog: *http://thecripplegate.com*.

Johnson, Jesse. "Dispensationalism, Keller, and the Poor", Aug. 16, 2011. Blog: *http://thecripplegate.com*.

Kurian, G. T. (2001). *Nelson's new Christian dictionary: the authoritative resource on the Christian world*. Nashville, TN: Thomas Nelson Publishers.

Leeman, Jonathan. (2010). *The Church and the Surprising Offense of God's Love: Reintroducing the Doctrines of Church Membership and Discipline*. Wheaton, IL: Crossway Books.

Lloyd-Jones, D. M. (2000). *Authentic Christianity*. Wheaton, IL: Crossway Books.

Norman, R. S. (2005). *The Baptist Way: Distinctives of a Baptist Church*. Nashville, TN: Broadman & Holman Publishers.

Reid, D. G., R. D. Linder, B. L. Shelley, and H. S. Stout. (1990). *Dictionary of Christianity in America*. Downers Grove, IL: InterVarsity Press.

Ryrie, C. C. (2010). *Dr. Ryrie's Articles*. Bellingham, WA: Logos Bible Software.

Vlach, Michael. (2008). *Dispensationalism: Essential Beliefs and Common Myths*. Theological Studies Press.

Vlach, Michael. (2010). *Has the Church Replaced Israel?* B & H Academic.

Books and articles which address missions and cultural issues related to the Southeast Asian context:

Bowers, Russell. (2003). *Folk Buddhism in Southeast Asia*. Training of Timothys.

Brinkley, Joel. (2012). *Cambodia's Curse: the Modern History of a Troubled Land*. Public Affairs.

Cormack, Don. (2009). *Killing Fields, Living Fields*. Christian Focus Press, reprint edition.

Davis, John. (1993). *Poles Apart: Contextualizing the Gospel in Asia.* Theological Book Trust.

Davis, John. (1997). *The Path to Enlightenment: Introducing Buddhism.* Hodder and Stoughton.

Fressanges, Alain. (2010). *Khmer Sayings.* Phnom Penh: KCD Publishing.

Hattaway, Paul. (2004). *The Peoples of the Buddhist World.* Piquant Editions.

McPhail, Forrest and Theo van Reijn. "Reaching Buddhists and Agnostics" *Sowing and Reaping,* July-August 2012. (See also: *http://www.gfamissions. org/resources/sowing-and-reaping.html*).

Smith, Alex. (2009). *Christian's Pocket Guide to Buddhism.* Christian Focus Publications.

Further Resources on the Web

http://www.cambodianchristianresources.com/missionary-resources/
This site seeks to provide a place for Christian workers in Cambodia to find resources for ministry among Cambodians. There are a number of helpful articles dealing with religion and methodology here as well.

http://dahlfred.com/index.php/blogs/gleanings-from-the-field
Overseas Missionary Fellowship missionary to Thailand, Karl Dahlfred, provides a number of helpful blog posts dealing with ministry in Thailand. Karl currently teaches part-time at Bangkok Bible Seminary and assists with editing and translation of Thai Christian books at Kanok Bannasan (OMF Publishers Thailand).

http://joshuaproject.net/joshua-project.php
This is easily the best resource for research about people groups and language groups available. They also provide many helps for learning where the greatest needs for the Gospel are in the world today.

http://www.mikevlach.com
This is the blog of Dr. Michael Vlach, Professor of Theology at The Master's Seminary in Sun Valley, California. Dr. Vlach specializes in the areas of Systematic Theology, Historical Theology, Apologetics, and World Religions. His specific area of expertise concerns the nation Israel and issues related to refuting the doctrine of Replacement Theology.

http://www.missionfrontiers.org/blog
Mission Frontiers is dedicated to fostering and supporting a global movement to establish indigenous and self-reproducing church planting movements among the 10,000 unreached peoples (ethnic groups) of the world.

http://missionsmandate.org/
Missions Mandate is a website in conjunction with Student Global Impact and Detroit Baptist Theological Seminary, ministries of Inter-City Baptist Church in Allen Park, MI.

http://www.sermonaudio.com/source_articles.asp?sourceid=forrestmcphail
This site is primarily dedicated to sermon and resources in the Khmer/Cambodian language, but there are also a number of helpful articles on missionary methodology there as well.

http://www.vulnerablemission.org/
Vulnerable Mission is dedicated to encouraging genuinely indigenous ministries in Africa. They seek to influence foreign missionaries to commit to learning African languages and culture and see the work of the Gospel go forward without foreign financial subsidy.

http://wmausa.org/
World Missions Associates, founded by Glenn Schwartz, has as its purpose "Intentionally integrating Biblical principles and best practices for local-sustainability and multiplication in global missions." This organization is also dedicated to helping churches around the world that are in dependence upon foreign subsidy to become self-sustaining.

About the Author

Forrest grew up in the Chicago, IL, area. He and his wife, Jennifer, have four children. They arrived in Cambodia, Southeast Asia, as church planting missionaries in 2000. Forrest has had opportunities to write articles for various smaller publications and has served as an adjunct professor for the missions program at Bob Jones University in Greenville, SC. They love the Khmer language, Cambodian culture, and are grateful to God for the privilege of serving Him in Southeast Asia.

Made in the USA
Charleston, SC
10 August 2015